Entrepreneurship
QUIZZES

12 EASY TESTS TO HELP YOU BECOME SUCCESSFULLY SELF-EMPLOYED

JOHN J. LIPTAK, ED.D.

JIST Works
America's Career Publisher

Entrepreneurship Quizzes
12 Easy Tests to Help You Become Successfully Self-Employed

© 2012 by John J. Liptak

Published by JIST Works, an imprint of JIST Publishing
875 Montreal Way
St. Paul, MN 55102
E-mail: info@jist.com

Visit our website at **www.jist.com** for information on JIST, free job search tips, tables of contents, sample pages, and ordering instructions for our many products!

Acquisitions/Development Editor: Heather Stith
Copy Editor: Colleen Totz Diamond
Production Editor: Jeanne Clark
Production Manager: Timothy W. Larson
Cover and Interior Designers: Aleata Halbig/Timothy W. Larson
Proofreader: Laura Bowman
Indexer: Kelly D. Henthorne

Printed in the United States of America
18 17 16 15 14 13 12   9 8 7 6 5 4 3 2 1

Library of Congress Cataloging-in-Publication data is on file with the Library of Congress.

ISBN 978-1-59357-919-7

The Ticket to Becoming Your Own Boss

Congratulations! You are embarking on a journey that will undoubtedly be the most exciting and challenging venture of your life and career. This book is designed to help you reach the pinnacle of career success—entrepreneurship.

Entrepreneurship has become one of the most dynamic forces in the economy and the driving force for much of the world's economic growth. Entrepreneurs are people who innovate and create new products and services and provide them on demand for the general public. They are multitalented individuals who have the ability to perceive opportunities where others cannot.

If you want to join the growing numbers of people who are saying goodbye to traditional jobs and starting and maintaining their own businesses, this book can guide you toward making it happen. Through a series of 12 simple quizzes and several follow-up exercises, it will help you

- Explore your readiness to begin your own business

- Identify business ideas based on your passions and talents

- Map out a plan to implement your idea

- Develop a skill set that is critical for entrepreneurial success

Beginning your own business is not easy. But the benefits of entrepreneurship—independence and control over your own business, the possibility of making a difference in the lives of others, a chance to reach your full career potential, and an opportunity to make a lot of money—make it a risk worth taking. By the time you finish the activities in this book, you will be well on your way to owning and operating your own thriving business.

Acknowledgments

Writing the third book in this series (the first and second being *Career Quizzes* and *College Major Quizzes*) has been an experience that I will treasure forever. Because I have gone through the trials and tribulations of starting and growing my own business, this book has been a labor of love. First and foremost, my deepest gratitude goes to the budding entrepreneurs with whom I have had the pleasure to work. Thank you for letting me be a part of your entrepreneurial start-ups and for trusting me to share your stories, dreams, hardships, and successes. You have taught me much about the skills necessary to start and grow your own business. I will be forever grateful.

I want to thank the following people for their generous contributions during the writing of this book. Most importantly, I would like to thank my fantastic editor at JIST Publishing, Heather Stith, for her attention to details, constructive suggestions, creativity, and steadfast devotion to this project. I am grateful for her skillful editorial direction, friendship, and intuitive insights. Her feedback and editorial talents are greatly appreciated.

I would also like to thank Sue Pines, Associate Publisher at JIST Publishing, who understood the promise of this book from the beginning. I appreciate how she embraced this project with gusto. Without her encouragement and support, this book would not have been possible. I am indebted to her for believing in me, wisely advising me during this project, and inspiring my best work.

Finally, I would like to thank my wife, Kathy, who has supported me during the writing of this book. I love her very much and I owe her a special debt of gratitude for her support, patience, and encouragement.

Table of Contents

Part 4: Developing Entrepreneurial Skills

Introduction

"After studying millionaires for more than twenty years, I have concluded that if you make one major decision correctly, you can become economically productive. If you are creative enough to select the ideal vocation, you can win, win big-time. The really brilliant millionaires are those who selected a vocation that they love—one that has few competitors but generates high profits."

—Thomas J. Stanley, author of *The Millionaire Mind* (Andrews McMeel Publishing, 2000)

Before the birth of industrialization and assembly lines, most people worked for themselves making a living or exchanging services for goods they did not have. As people find less fulfillment in their work and have increasingly limited opportunities for advancement, they are finding ways to get back to entrepreneurial careers. Entrepreneurship provides an opportunity for self-expression, self-fulfillment, and self-sufficiency.

If you have ever wanted to be your own boss or felt tired of working and making money for other people, this book might just be what you are looking for. Entrepreneurship requires introspection, imagination, goal setting, and an action-oriented business plan. This book will help you with all of these things.

My Life as an Entrepreneur

I work as a counselor in a small college in Virginia. I am competent at my job and perform it to the best of my abilities every day. But it is through an activity that I pursue in my spare time that I am able to receive the majority of my professional satisfaction and be an entrepreneur.

My interest in self-exploration assessments first developed when I was working on my dissertation as part of the requirements for completing my Doctor of Education degree at Virginia Tech. For my dissertation, I decided to create an interest assessment that would help other people assess their interests in work, leisure, and learning situations. I thought it was a good dissertation, but I never thought of it as a product I could sell until I found a publisher, JIST Publishing, that agreed to publish it and pay me a percentage of the profits. I agreed and figured I would make a couple of bucks from the deal. To my surprise, JIST Publishing sold nearly two million copies of the assessment instrument (and it continues to sell!), and I was encouraged to develop more assessments. From this experience, I learned that I had a talent for developing self-exploration materials and that it was an activity I enjoyed. I wondered if I could turn this activity into an entrepreneurial venture.

I always had thought I had all the qualities of a great entrepreneur: I was creative, ambitious, hard-working, self-motivated, and structured. But I wasn't sure whether I really had what was necessary to succeed in my own business. I decided to do a little research to find out. I searched all of the entrepreneurship websites and books I could find. I found plenty of information to help me succeed in developing a business plan, choosing a business to offer, and marketing my business. What I was unable to find was information that could help me to explore whether I had what it took to even venture out into the world of self-employment. Who could tell me if I was cut out to be an entrepreneur and whether I would be successful?

I finally decided that because I seemed to be so proficient in developing assessments, I would develop an assessment that I could take to see whether I had the qualities and skills that are necessary to become an entrepreneur. Since that time, I have used this assessment to help other people decide if they had the makings of an entrepreneur as well.

Upon administering the assessment to a variety of people interested in starting and owning their own business, I had many requests for other assessments that could help prospective entrepreneurs as well as seasoned entrepreneurs learn more about themselves and how they approach entrepreneurship. I discovered that an approach in which people completed an assessment prior to developing another aspect of their business greatly enhanced their probabilities of success. This book is the outcome of all of the assessments used to help prospective entrepreneurs begin, maintain, and grow their own businesses.

I have been where you are now, and I have seen my business grow over time. Many of my assessments have sold more than a million copies worldwide, and I continue to get requests to develop assessments for corporations and nonprofit agencies. I had my doubts about my ability to be a successful entrepreneur, but with patience and persistence I have been able to overcome obstacles and create a business that provides me with independence and a sense of purpose.

Entrepreneurship and Wealth

All of the research that has been completed on wealth in America suggests that the one sure way to both achieve freedom at work and make a lot of money is to start your own business.

In the blockbuster book *The Millionaire Next Door*, authors Thomas J. Stanley and William D. Danko provide a picture of most millionaires living in the United States. Their research is the most comprehensive ever conducted on the people who are wealthy in America and how they got that way. Some of their findings will amaze you:

- Two-thirds of the millionaires surveyed are self-employed. Self-employed people make up less than 20 percent of the workers in America but account for two-thirds of the millionaires. Three out of four of them who are self-employed consider themselves to be entrepreneurs; the others are self-employed service providers.

- Usually, millionaires are business people who have lived in the same town for all of their adult lives. These people own a small factory, a chain of stores, farms, or a service business.

- Self-employed people are four times more likely to be millionaires than those who work for others.

- The characteristics of the business owners are more important in predicting their level of wealth than the type of business they own.

- Most millionaires would not encourage their children to take over their business. Instead, most millionaires encourage their children to become self-employed professionals or small-business owners.

Many people think that entrepreneurs do what they do mostly to make a lot of money. Of course, entrepreneurs certainly are very much interested in making a lot of money (that's how they become millionaires), and they do enjoy having no limits on the amount of money they can make. But there's more to them than that.

They are a unique breed who

- Need to feel a sense of purpose or direction in what they are doing.

- Are willing to take calculated risks in order for their dreams to become a reality.

- Love to look for new business opportunities.

- Have an insatiable need for autonomy and independence.

- Are comfortable with uncertainty.

For entrepreneurs, starting a business is just as much about being passionate, autonomous, and obsessed with getting an idea to market as it is about making money. Entrepreneurs enjoy the freedom of being their own boss, believe that working for themselves is actually less risky than working for someone else, and like controlling their own destiny. Therefore, entrepreneurship is about developing a specific mindset and spirit, as well as developing entrepreneurial skills.

Characteristics of the New Entrepreneur

My parents had always stressed that career advancement with a large corporation was the way to attain success and happiness in American culture. This career advancement usually means getting as much education as you possibly can, working hard, working overtime and on weekends, changing jobs often, climbing a corporate "ladder," and having a good attitude about work or a Protestant work ethic. This dream of success, based on the idea of a linear career and catering to the organizations that shape careers, has provided the framework for the American values of individual accomplishment, competition, personal responsibility, and success at all costs. However, these notions of success seem to be changing.

I consider myself to be one of a new breed of entrepreneurs who are defining success on our own terms. Our notion of success dictates how many of us choose the work we do, how we spend our leisure time, when we marry, where we live, when we choose to have children, and the values and attitudes that we teach our children.

Several characteristics make the new entrepreneurs able to flourish in a society fraught with chaos and change. These characteristics are described in the following sections.

Do Not Be Content with Nine to Five

For the new entrepreneurs, "work" is what they do to earn money and make a living. For them, work provides the basic necessities, but not the challenge, autonomy, or fulfillment they want. The new entrepreneurs are less content than they used to be, and they want more out of life than the drudgery of a nine-to-five existence. Many are starting to see the negatives of working for someone else and seeing the positives of working for themselves. Creating their own business provides them with the greatest opportunities for financial, personal, and emotional success. They are demanding a work situation in which there are intrinsic rewards such as an opportunity to be creative, to have fun, to be enthusiastic, to take risks, and to use all of their energies. Only through entrepreneurship can they (and you) have it all!

Have the Best of Both Worlds

Companies are downsizing, streamlining operations, forcing early retirement, not replacing workers who retire or leave, and making life rough for all employees. In today's economy, no job is ever safe. The new entrepreneurs know this, but they recognize that they can have the best of both worlds. They can keep their full-time job to continue earning a living, but they can also start a business in their spare time.

Have Unlimited Possibilities

The new entrepreneurs know that working for big business is not where the opportunities are. People are no longer becoming slaves to big business for work. Instead, they are finding jobs in small companies that encourage flexibility.

Self-employment also is flourishing, and more and more people are jumping on the entrepreneurship bandwagon. People are no longer dependent on a robust economy to achieve their entrepreneurial dreams. They are creating their own businesses without large amounts of capital, in which they can use all of their talents and develop something that is truly their own.

Do Not Fear Downsizing

Unemployment is one of the most stressful events in a person's life. Research related to job loss indicates that the stress of unemployment can be linked to a variety of psychological disorders, including depression, anxiety, suicide, alcoholism, and child abuse. To make the situation even worse, factors such as these then interfere with the job search process. For people whose identity is tied to the work they do, the loss of that job often means the loss of identity or sense of self.

The new entrepreneurs do not fear being downsized because they have more than one source of income. They also know that it is dangerous to identify too much with their work because they can get complacent and reluctant to take the calculated risks associated with entrepreneurship.

Don't Worry About the Corporate Family

The workplace in countries around the world is changing so drastically that, unfortunately, work no longer provides people with the type of security that it did 30 or even 20 years ago. No longer do people have the luxury of working at a job all of their lives, and most do not feel like they are part of the corporate "family." No longer can people depend on their work to meet anything but a person's most basic needs. No longer are people guaranteed promotions and pay raises based on their performance at work. For some, work is no longer even available, regardless of educational attainment level or the amount of work experience. More people are working longer and harder just to keep up.

In addition to many people losing their jobs, other major changes have occurred in the workplace that make work less secure for many people. Wages over the last decade have steadily declined for the average worker. In addition, compensation plans have been affected so that employers are paying less toward employee pension plans and health insurance costs and employees are paying more for these benefits.

Some changes in the workplace are positive. Technology is driving many of the new opportunities in the world of work. Development of computer technology has made it possible for everyone to have inexpensive access to tons of information and the ability to create it and utilize it from almost anywhere.

The new entrepreneurs are quite comfortable with change and a lack of security in the workplace. They have seen their parents lose jobs due to downsizing and restructuring, thus they have come to see job change as a necessary ingredient of career development. They are not afraid because they have an ace in the hole—a small business of their very own. They believe that there are no more guarantees in the workplace and are able to live with that knowledge. Because they are not interested in "climbing the corporate ladder," they see no need to stay at one job for their entire career. They look at job-hopping as a way of building skills and maintaining their participation in interesting leisure activities. Thus, a job to them is merely a way to make money to support their real interest—their own business.

Think Opportunistically

The new entrepreneurs like to create new and innovative products and services that get the world excited. They are not afraid to bend the rules to get an innovative product or service to their customers. They see opportunities and possibilities all around them just waiting to be exploited—and needs waiting to be filled. They are creative and innovative and willing to take calculated risks. Most entrepreneurs are risk takers, but new entrepreneurs want to ensure that the gambles they take are buffered by the fact that they maintain their steady incomes until their business is profitable. They are able to assess their options and choose the best course of action for success. They are not afraid to fail because they have little to lose and always learn from their mistakes.

The New Entrepreneur Inventory

Take the following quick assessment to help determine if you are a new entrepreneur.

1. I am not content working a typical nine-to-five day.	True False
2. I believe that having my own business will provide me with personal and financial success.	True False
3. If I work for a corporation, it is just to make money.	True False
4. I want the financial security that my own business would provide.	True False
5. I need intrinsic rewards (creativity, autonomy, etc.) that a job does not provide.	True False
6. I am able to see opportunities where most people do not.	True False
7. I don't care about being part of a "corporate family."	True False
8. My work is no longer satisfying.	True False
9. I am comfortable with change.	True False
10. I am a risk taker.	True False

Add the total number of True answers that you circled. Then transfer your total to the space below.

New Entrepreneur Total: _____

Your score will help you gauge how well you fit into the new entrepreneur model. A score from 0 to 3 indicates that you will need to develop some skills to cultivate a new entrepreneur mindset. Don't despair, though, the remainder of this book will help you develop those skills.

A score from 4 to 6 indicates that you have developed some of the skills needed for a new entrepreneur mindset. Read on, and you will enhance your skills even more.

If you scored from 7 to 10, you have developed many of the skills needed for a new entrepreneur mindset. For you, the remainder of the book will help you to hone your skills even further.

The Method Used in This Book

People have relied on quizzes as a way of reflecting on their behavior, thoughts, and feelings to make educated decisions and implement their goals. This process of self-exploration began thousands of years ago, with an extraordinary Greek philosopher named Socrates. He believed that his mission was one of helping other people to seek a deeper understanding of what constituted a good life. He was dedicated to discovering wisdom within himself and drawing this wisdom out of others. His method, called the Socratic Method, consisted of a series of questions he would pose to help other people explore their true nature so they could experience success.

This book adheres to Socrates' mantra that "the unexamined life is not worth living." It will help you to examine and explore the enduring qualities or characteristics you possess and how those characteristics affect your career and your motivation to start your own business.

The Guided Self-Reflection Approach

Entrepreneurship Quizzes is unlike most other books that are designed to help you start your own business, largely because it does not pretend to provide you with a magic formula for success. You have to work for it by taking the 12 quizzes in the book.

But they aren't really quizzes (not in the panic-inducing, late-night-cramming sense of the word). They are self-assessments designed to help you explore your interests, skills, and other personal characteristics and then apply those characteristics to your choice of a business type. Quizzes can help you to recognize patterns of behavior, identify strategies that are productive and unproductive, and enrich your understanding of how you interact with the world. Quizzes provide a path to self-discovery through the exploration of your unique traits. I call this guided self-reflection.

Guided self-reflection is a unique way of learning about yourself. Each chapter of this book will coach you through the following self-reflection process:

- Assessing your readiness to begin your own business

- Exploring the type of business you might want to start

- Evaluating the comprehensiveness of the business plan for your business

- Judging your ability to manage your time, money, and stress

The quizzes in this book will help you see yourself as you really are, though be aware that they are exercises in self-exploration and not final definitions of your character or attitudes. Still, the results of this process should help you to reflect on your life, question past behaviors, find meaning, and make connections. You will be encouraged to make specific plans, set goals, and take action. After all, *that* is the point of this book. The quizzes are simply a way of getting there.

A Word About the Quizzes in this Book

A quiz can provide you with valuable information about yourself. However, please remember that such instruments cannot measure everything about you. The purpose of these quizzes is not to pigeonhole you, but to allow you to explore your personal preferences and characteristics and how they impact your career development. Remember too that this book contains *quizzes* and not *tests,* at least not in the traditional sense. Traditional tests measure knowledge or whether something is right or wrong. For the exercises in this book, there are no right or wrong answers. These quizzes only ask for your opinions or attitudes about issues that are critical in entrepreneurship.

Also keep in mind that the quizzes in the book are based on self-reported data. In other words, the accuracy and usefulness of the information is dependent on the information that you provide about yourself. You may not learn much from taking some of these assessments, or you might verify information that you already know. On the other hand, you may uncover information that might be keeping you from being as happy or as successful as you might be.

All of the quizzes in this book are designed to be administered, scored, and interpreted by you. They are merely a starting point for you to begin learning more about yourself and how you fit into the world. You may not always agree with the outcomes of all inventories. Do not get upset. Remember that this is merely an exploratory exercise and not a final definition of who you are or what you believe. Lastly, the quizzes are not a substitute for professional assistance. If you feel you need additional help, please consult a career counselor or small business professional.

As you complete the quizzes in this book, remember to do the following:

- Take your time completing them. There is no time limit, so work at your own pace. Allow yourself time to reflect on your results and how they compare to what you already know about yourself.

- Do not answer the quiz questions as you think others would like you to answer them or how you think others see you. Remember that these assessments are for you to reflect on your life and explore some of the barriers that are keeping you from attaining career success.

- Honestly complete the exercises that are included after each quiz. These exercises will allow you to explore how the results of each assessment can be integrated into your personal and career development.

- Find a quiet place where you can complete the quizzes without being disturbed.

- Quizzes are powerful tools—so long as you are honest with yourself. Take your time and be truthful in your responses so that your results are an honest reflection of *you*. Your level of commitment in completing the quizzes will determine the levels of success that you achieve.

- Before completing each quiz, be sure to read the instructions. All of the quizzes have similar formats, but they have different scales, responses, scoring instructions, and methods for interpretation.

- Remember that learning about yourself should be *fun*. Don't stress over the quizzes or the results. Just learn as much about yourself as you can.

Remember that anyone can start their own business, but it does require some work on your part. This book is designed to walk you through a tried-and-true process for successfully starting and growing your own business. Be faithful to the process and you will be rewarded by identifying, developing, implementing, and succeeding in your own business.

PART 1: PREPARING FOR ENTREPRENEURSHIP

"Entrepreneurs average 3.8 failures before final success. What sets the successful ones apart is their amazing persistence."

—Lisa M. Amos

CHAPTER 1

Evaluate Your Mindset

Congratulations! By considering the possibility of starting your own business, you are embarking on a journey that will undoubtedly be the most exciting of your life and career. Entrepreneurship is often the pinnacle of a person's career. One of the most important questions you need to ask yourself at this point is not "Am I cut out for this?" but rather "How am I cut out for this?" Entrepreneurship is not a DNA set that you either inherit or you don't. Anyone can be an entrepreneur. Determining how you would like to become an entrepreneur is a major career decision, however, and should not be taken lightly. Because entrepreneurship represents a critical juncture in your career, you need a plan for navigating the journey.

Many people realize (too late) that quitting their jobs and jumping into a full-time small business is a mistake. When you consider entrepreneurship, consider that people incorporate entrepreneurial ventures into their lives with varying levels of participation. For example, I work a full-time job in addition to running my business. I like the security of working for a corporation. I also like the security of knowing that if I ever do get downsized, I can simply work full-time at my business.

There are three basic levels of participation in entrepreneurial activity:

- Some entrepreneurs keep their full-time jobs and begin a part-time business in their spare time. This approach allows people to maintain a steady paycheck and benefits, career security, and the identity that goes along with working for someone else. In addition, this provides an opportunity to "try out" entrepreneurship and slowly build a business.

- Some entrepreneurs take part-time jobs that allow them to devote significant amounts of time to their entrepreneurial venture. This approach allows people to continue to make some money while they begin their entrepreneurial venture.

- Some entrepreneurs stop working for someone else and jump right into full-time entrepreneurship. This approach tends to be the riskiest route to take in beginning a business.

Beginning your own business requires that you make a significant change in your mindset, moving from a corporate mindset to an entrepreneurial mindset. People move from the corporate mindset to the entrepreneurial mindset at varying levels of intensity. The differences between the two mindsets are illustrated below:

Entrepreneurship Mindset	**Corporate Mindset**
Willing to take risks	Adverse to risk taking
Can go without pay if need be	Wants consistent paychecks
Values wealth over job security	Values job security over wealth
Long, often irregular hours	Regular, consistent hours
Copes easily with change	Resists change
Freedom to control direction of career/business	Has little or no say over direction of company
Potential for large payoff	Consistent pay regardless of work

The following assessment helps you explore the intensity of your level of motivation and determine whether you're ready to start your own business.

The Entrepreneurial Mindset Scale

This scale contains 35 statements that are divided into 5 sections. Read each statement and decide how true the statement is for you. Then circle the number in the appropriate column.

> 3 = True
>
> 2 = Somewhat True
>
> 1 = Not True

This is not a test. There are no right or wrong answers, so do not spend too much time thinking about your answers. Be sure to respond to every statement. Do not worry about totaling your scores at this point. Simply respond to the 35 statements.

	True	Somewhat True	Not True
1. I am not afraid of living on less money while a business grows.	3	2	1
2. I am convinced I could make a lot of money in my own business.	3	2	1
3. I am dissatisfied with my standard of living.	3	2	1
4. Money is more important to me than career satisfaction.	3	2	1
5. One of my career goals is to become wealthy.	3	2	1
6. Money is the only measure of a person's success.	3	2	1
7. I don't worry about financial security.	3	2	1
Section 1 Total: _____			
8. Autonomy is important to me.	3	2	1
9. I like being my own boss.	3	2	1
10. I prefer to work independently.	3	2	1
11. I like to direct my own work schedule.	3	2	1
12. Having coworkers is not important to me.	3	2	1
13. I can be productive in an unstructured environment.	3	2	1
14. I like to make my own decisions.	3	2	1
Section 2 Total: _____			
15. I have no desire to climb the corporate ladder.	3	2	1
16. I want to make decisions about my life and my business.	3	2	1
17. I do not want to wait for approval to do things anymore.	3	2	1
18. The structure of a corporate job stifles me.	3	2	1
19. I could accept not receiving a paycheck.	3	2	1
20. I hate corporate politics.	3	2	1
21. I hate to commute to and from work.	3	2	1
Section 3 Total: _____			
22. I am more ambitious than other people.	3	2	1
23. I want to be paid for what I'm worth.	3	2	1
24. I want to make money for myself, not someone else.	3	2	1
25. A steady paycheck is not essential to me.	3	2	1
26. I want to be rewarded for my hard work.	3	2	1
27. I am willing to take risks to be rewarded.	3	2	1
28. I want to make money based on my performance.	3	2	1
Section 4 Total: _____			

(continued)

(continued)

	True	Somewhat True	Not True
29. I would enjoy a flexible work schedule.	3	2	1
30. I want to work when I am most productive.	3	2	1
31. I want to decide where I work.	3	2	1
32. I want to create my own work schedule.	3	2	1
33. I enjoy working at times when most businesses are not open.	3	2	1
34. Working irregular hours doesn't bother me.	3	2	1
35. I need to work the hours I want to work.	3	2	1
Section 5 Total: _____			

Scoring

Determining whether you have an entrepreneurial mindset is critical in your success. Remember that you do not necessarily need to possess all of the aspects that comprise an entrepreneurial mindset. However, the more aspects of an entrepreneurial mindset that you possess, the more likely you are to succeed as a full-time entrepreneur. People possessing fewer aspects of an entrepreneurial mindset may be more successful by continuing to work at a job while beginning a business.

For each section below, count the scores you circled for the items. Then transfer your scores below:

Standard of Living (Section 1) Total: _____

Independence (Section 2) Total: _____

Tired of Corporate Life (Section 3) Total: _____

Benefits of Hard Work (Section 4) Total: _____

Flexibility (Section 5) Total: _____

For each of these sections, a score of 7–11 is considered low, a score of 12–16 is average, and a score of 17–21 is high. Now add up all the scores for all the sections to calculate your total entrepreneurial mindset. Write this number below:

Entrepreneurial Mindset Total: _____

A total score from 35 to 58 indicates that you possess some of the necessary qualities to be a successful entrepreneur, but maybe not enough to quit your job or quit looking for traditional employment opportunities. You will probably be most successful in a situation in which you can start a small business in your spare time without having to give up full-time employment.

If you scored in the average range (59–81), you may possess many entrepreneurial characteristics that could enhance the success of a small or home-based business. You may not be quite ready to quit your job, but you might consider working fewer hours so that you can devote more of your time to starting a small or home-based business. This combination of part-time traditional and entrepreneurial work will enable you to ensure a successful business start-up.

High scores—scores that range from 82 to 105—indicate that you probably possess enough entrepreneurial characteristics to own your own business. You will probably find tremendous career satisfaction through owning your own small or home-based business. You should begin to identify some potential entrepreneurial opportunities. Jumping right into entrepreneurship full-time is the riskiest approach, but it's not impossible. You will be taking a risk based on your faith in yourself, your unique business plan, and the skills you will learn throughout this book.

Making the Transition

Before you embark on your new life as an entrepreneur, you need to think about how you will transition from working in a traditional corporate job to working for yourself. For most entrepreneurs, this is a slow and calculated process. In the following worksheets, you can examine your feelings about making this transition. For each of the mindset sections that follow, write about how the change from a corporate mindset to an entrepreneurial mindset makes you feel. For sections in which you scored in the average or low range, you should explore what aspects of the corporate mindset you are reluctant to let go. For the scales on which you scored in the high range, explore how your entrepreneurial mindset is driving you to begin your own business.

Standard of Living

High scores on this section suggest that you are ready to determine your own standard of living, not one dictated by a supervisor in a corporate job. You believe that you can make more money in your own business, and you are willing to risk going without a paycheck in order to have a higher standard of living in the future.

Feelings About Your Standard of Living

Corporation

Your standard of living is set for you in terms of your weekly or monthly paycheck, after which raises are at the whim of the employer.

Entrepreneurship

Your standard of living is determined by how successful you are in promoting and selling a product or service.

Notes:

_____

_____

_____

_____

Independence

High scores on this section suggest that you are ready to work independently and to start and grow your business. You are interested in making your own decisions and deciding which direction your business takes. You want to be able to be independent and not wait for supervisors to assign and approve your work.

Feelings About Independence

Corporation

Your supervisor assigns you work and you complete the work how and when it is specified by the supervisor.

Entrepreneurship

You decide what you want to work on and when you want to complete it. You control how your own business is run.

Notes:

_____

_____

_____

_____

Tired of Corporate Life

High scores on this scale suggest that you are tired of living the corporate life—the commute, corporate clothing, and having to ask for vacation time off. You no longer want to worry about impressing supervisors and coworkers. You no longer want to work corporate hours and deal with corporate politics.

Feelings About Corporate Life

Corporation

You are eligible to climb the career ladder. If you choose to, you will have to endure corporate politics and work based on the rules of the corporation.

Entrepreneurship

No career ladder exists for you to climb, and you'll encounter very little politics. You determine what needs to be done and how you complete the work.

Notes:

_____

_____

_____

_____

Benefits of Hard Work

High scores on this scale suggest that you are tired of working to make money for other people—owners of the corporation and your supervisors. You want to be paid for what you are worth and how much value you bring to the organization. You want to profit when the corporation profits.

Feelings About the Benefits of Hard Work

Corporation

You are paid a salary and benefits in exchange for work. You do not benefit when profits soar, and you are not paid more for hard work.

Entrepreneurship

You are paid according to how much work you complete in terms of selling your product or service. Your profits usually rise as your hard work rises.

Notes:

_____

_____

Flexibility

High scores on this scale suggest that you want to work how, when, and where you want to work. You are tired of being forced to produce your best work during the hours of 9 to 5. You do not always work most effectively during those hours. You want to have some flexibility in determining how you do your work.

Feelings About Flexibility

Corporation

You work 9 to 5 and some evenings and weekends to complete your work.

Entrepreneurship

You work when, how, and where you work most effectively.

Notes:

_____

_____

_____

Redesigning Your Lifestyle

Now that you are considering entrepreneurship, you need to redesign your career and life to embrace entrepreneurship. This may require making some changes in your lifestyle. Everyone moves into the world of entrepreneurship at a different rate and in a different way. You should not push yourself into entrepreneurship before you are ready. You should rely on your scores on the assessment in this chapter to gauge the rate at which to enter entrepreneurship, and then design a plan for integrating entrepreneurship into your life and career.

You may want to integrate entrepreneurship into your life for a number of reasons:

- People who are entrepreneurs are more in control of their careers and their lives.

- People who have the most fulfilling careers often have multiple income-producing opportunities.

- People who are happiest create financially rewarding activities.

- People who are happiest often work for someone else while maintaining a loyalty and commitment to themselves through entrepreneurship.

- People who begin entrepreneurial ventures while still maintaining a job have the most career security.

Entrepreneurship makes additional demands on your time and energy. Therefore, before you begin planning and developing your business, you need to see how entrepreneurship is going to affect your life and the lives of people around you. The following exercises are designed to help you explore how your life will be different if you decide to start your own business.

Time

To begin, let's explore how much time you are devoting to current life roles and responsibilities. Explore how much time you devote to various roles and activities in your life.

Analyzing Your Time

In the spaces that follow, break down how much time you spend in each role you play during a typical week. Fill in the "other" category with specific activities related to your life. Therefore, a person who spends time each week volunteering at the animal shelter could simply write "volunteering" in that space. To get an accurate picture of how you spend your time each week, I suggest keeping a daily journal. At the end of each day, reflect back on how you spent your time, and then record those activities in your journal. At the end of the week, you will need to calculate the number of hours you spend engaging in the activities in the various roles.

Activities in Roles I Play	*Time Spent in Activity Each Week*
Working at my job	_____
Commuting to work	_____
Working around the house	_____
Family activities	_____
Caring for family	_____
Sleeping	_____
Eating	_____
Engaging in hobbies	_____
Religious/spiritual activities	_____
Playing/watching sports	_____
Other: _____	_____

Given your current schedule, how much time per week do you currently have for beginning your own business? How will you spend that time?

_____

_____

(continued)

Analyzing Your Time (continued)

In the following spaces, block out the days and the times that you will have available to work on beginning your business:

Days of the Week	Time I Will Work on My Business
Monday	Monday House Business
Tuesday	
Wednesday	
Thursday	
Friday	
Saturday	
Sunday	

How many hours per week will you have to devote to starting your own business?

_____

Is this enough time, or not enough?

_____

What will you need to cut out of your current schedule to have more time to devote to beginning/growing your business?

_____

_____

How will this affect others in your life?

_____

_____

_____

Energy

Starting your own business requires you to have extra reserves of energy. You will need to examine how much energy you are also devoting to the various roles and activities in your life.

Analyzing Your Energy

In the spaces that follow, break down how much energy you spend in each role you play during a typical week. Fill in the "other" category with a specific activity related to your life, such as volunteering. Use the following categories to record the amount of energy you are exerting: a lot, some, a little, very little, or none. Again, keeping a daily journal in which you can document how much energy you are spending in each activity will help you to complete this worksheet. At the end of the week, evaluate the amount of energy you spend engaging in the activities in the various roles.

Activities in Roles I Play

Activities in Roles I Play	*Energy Spent in Activity*
Working at my job	_____
Commuting to work	_____
Working around the house	_____
Family activities	_____
Caring for family	_____
Sleeping	_____
Eating	_____
Engaging in hobbies	_____
Religious/spiritual activities	_____
Playing/watching sports	_____
Other: _____	_____

Given your current schedule, how much energy per week do you currently have for beginning your own business? How will you use that energy?

_____

_____

In the following spaces, block out the days and the times that you will have available to work on beginning your business:

(continued)

Analyzing Your Energy (continued)

Days of the Week	*Times I Will Have Energy to Work on My Business*
Monday	_____
Tuesday	_____
Wednesday	_____
Thursday	_____
Friday	_____
Saturday	_____
Sunday	_____

How much energy per week will you have to devote to starting your own business?

_____

Is this enough energy?

_____

What will you need to cut out of your current schedule to have more energy to devote to beginning/growing your business?

_____

_____

How will this affect others in your life?

_____

_____

_____

Relationships

Given that starting your own business will greatly affect the relationships in your life and career, it is important to explore how starting a business will affect the significant people in your life.

Considering Your Relationships

List the people who can help you to begin your business and describe how they can help:

Person Who Can Help

How He or She Can Help

chanis

How will beginning your own business affect your family life?

The purpose of this chapter is to help you examine your readiness to start and grow a business. All people are not going to start their businesses the same way. Some will want to continue working full-time while their business gets off the ground (like me!), while others will want to jump right in and begin promoting their product or service as quickly as they can. You need to remember that you will need available resources, time, and energy to start your business venture. The next chapter will address fears that you may be having about starting your own business.

CHAPTER 2

Overcome Your Fears

You may experience many doubts and fears about pursuing an entrepreneurial venture. Experiencing these fears is natural and to be expected.

Although you will face many challenges when you start your own business, the most critical roadblocks you will face are the ones that are inside your head. These fears and doubts take on a life of their own when you begin to think about starting a business. When I developed the *Career Exploration Inventory*, my first career assessment, many negative thoughts repeatedly streamed through my mind. "What if people laugh at my idea?" and "Assessments are only used for psychiatric problems" were two of the most prominent ones.

The secret of being a successful entrepreneur lies in facing your fears rather than letting them act as an excuse for not reaching your full potential as an entrepreneur. If you continue to say to yourself things such as "I'm not quite ready yet, but someday I will do it," you're listening to your fears.

Most of the fears you're experiencing are probably related to transitioning from corporate life to entrepreneurial life. Whether you lack confidence, social support, finances, or any of the other areas measured on the Entrepreneurial Fears Scale, those fears are tied directly to the lack of job security that accompanies beginning your own business.

Remember that experiencing these feelings is natural. All people want the security and steady paycheck a corporate job provides; however, entrepreneurs take risks to find fulfillment and freedom in their businesses. If down deep in your soul you believe that you were born to be an entrepreneur, you cannot let your fears rule your career decisions. The assessment and exercises in this chapter will help you to identify and overcome the fears that are holding you back from the exciting life of entrepreneurship.

Facing the Fear of Failure

Fear of failure is a strong deterrent for many people interested in starting a business. Before I developed the *Career Exploration Inventory* for publication, I had several other business ideas that I thought would be successful. However, I let other people (and myself) talk me out of taking my ideas to market. I eventually saw some of those ideas come to market only to make a lot of money for other people.

Then one day, I simply got tired of seeing other people profit from ideas that I already had. I was watching a golf tournament on television and I saw a NIKE commercial that ended with the words "Just Do It!" These three simple words resonated with me, and I could not get them out of my head. I was going to just do it. Those three words seemed to set my entrepreneurial soul free to stop worrying about what other people might say. I finally asked myself, "What is the worst thing that could happen?" My answer was, "The publishers could say no." I decided I could live with that.

If You Are Like Me . . .

Here are some reasons why you, like me, may choose to overcome your fears:

- Trying and not being successful is better than never trying at all.
- You do not want to sell your legacy short, and starting a small business would be a great addition to your legacy.
- You don't want to say at the end of your life, "I wish I had. . . ."
- You are tired of making money for a large corporation, tired of working structured hours, and tired of taking orders from a supervisor who knows less than you.

The key to overcoming your fear of failure when starting your own business is to accept that failure is a part of life for entrepreneurs—and keep going. Entrepreneurs are a rare breed of people who simply keep trying until they find success. Most entrepreneurs have failed several times, but they typically see their failures as a learning process. For some entrepreneurs, failure can also be a motivator and fuel for success.

I certainly have learned a great deal from my failures. My view is that if one idea fails, I'll simply try another until I find one that hits big. My first published assessment was rejected by 10 publishers before finally being published. If I had let my fears and doubts get in the way, I would have simply given up. Don't make the mistake of giving up before you even get started!

Prepare for success. You will need to learn as much as you possibly can about yourself and about developing and implementing a business plan. This book is designed to help you learn about yourself through a series of interrelated quizzes.

This book will also help you to develop a comprehensive business plan for implementing your business.

By using the information that you learn in this book, you will be empowered to make informed decisions about the feasibility of any new business start-up you are considering. This feeling of empowerment will in turn provide you with the self-confidence you need to overcome the fears you might be feeling about starting your own business.

The Entrepreneurial Fears Scale

This assessment is designed to help you explore the major fears you have about owning and operating your own business. This assessment contains 30 statements that are related to the fears most entrepreneurs have in starting and owning a business. Read each of the statements and decide whether the statement describes you. If the statement does describe you, circle the number in the True column. If the statement does not describe you, circle the number in the False column.

This is not a test. There are no right or wrong answers, so do not spend too much time thinking about your answers. Be sure to respond to every statement.

	True	False
1. I believe I can start my own business.	2	1
2. I'm not very competitive in business.	1	2
3. I consider myself a trailblazer in business.	2	1
4. I do not have confidence in my ability to start a new business.	1	2
5. I have skills that would be in demand in my own business.	2	1
Section 1 Total: _____		
6. I don't have people with whom to share my entrepreneurial. successes and failures.	1	2
7. I'm aware how entrepreneurship will affect my family life.	2	1
8. I have friends and family who will help me succeed.	2	1
9. I don't have anyone to talk to about my business ideas.	1	2
10. Having a support system is over-rated.	1	2
Section 2 Total: _____		

(continued)

(continued)

		True	False
11.	I have no idea about what kind of business I could start.	1	2
12.	I see business opportunities everywhere.	2	1
13.	I do not know what type of business to begin.	1	2
14.	I'm sure my business idea will work.	2	1
15.	I am able to see how to improve on existing products/services.	2	1
	Section 3 Total: _____		
16.	I'm not afraid of living on less money while a business grows.	2	1
17.	The cost of starting a business scares me.	1	2
18.	I need the benefits that accompany a job.	1	2
19.	I like having a steady paycheck.	1	2
20.	I trust in my ability to make a living from my own business.	2	1
	Section 4 Total: _____		
21.	I'm taking a big financial risk in starting a business.	1	2
22.	I worry about the legal problems that accompany a new business.	1	2
23.	I'm convinced I could make a lot of money in my own business.	2	1
24.	I'm willing to start my business in my spare time to save money.	2	1
25.	I know where I can get money to begin my own business.	2	1
	Section 5 Total: _____		
26.	A small business would take all of my time.	1	2
27.	I feel like I would get consumed by my own business.	1	2
28.	I'm able to maintain my priorities.	2	1
29.	I would be able to balance entrepreneurship and other things in life.	2	1
30.	I would get obsessed with making my business a success.	1	2
	Section 6 Total: _____		

Scoring

The assessment is designed to measure the level of your fears related to starting and owning your own business. To get your score, total the numbers you circled for True statements in each of the sections. Put that number on the "Total" line following each section. You will get a score from 5 to 10. Then transfer your scores to the lines that follow:

Confidence (Section 1) Total: _____

Support (Section 2) Total: _____

Ideas (Section 3) Total: _____

Job Security (Section 4) Total: _____

Finances (Section 5) Total: _____

Balance (Section 6) Total: _____

Scores from 5 to 6 in a section indicate that you have significant fears in this area about starting your own business. This chapter includes exercises and activities to help you overcome these fears.

Scores from 7 to 8 indicate that you have some fears in this area about starting your own business. This chapter includes exercises and activities to help you overcome these fears.

Scores from 9 to 10 indicate that you do not have many fears in this area about starting your own business. However, the exercises and activities in this chapter can help you be even more confident in starting your own business.

Building Confidence

Entrepreneurship can help you overcome your doubts and fears and provide you with a newfound sense of purpose. Fears have a way of blocking your natural passion about your idea, product, or service. Most unsuccessful entrepreneurs fail because their fears prevent them from getting their ideas to market, not because they have a bad idea for their business.

In most cases, the process goes something like this:

1. You have a great idea that you believe nobody has thought about before. You develop the idea in your mind.

2. You begin to get your idea down on paper. You sketch it out, think about names, and begin to define your sales market.

3. You do a little preliminary research about who might be interested in helping you develop your project. You envision all of the great ways that you can market your product or service and develop your brand.

Now you begin to have doubts about your idea or project. You say things to yourself like "It will interfere with my job" or "It would take up too much of my time." You also begin to hear other people say things like "That idea is crazy." By the time these internal thoughts stream through your mind multiple times, and external negative statements hit home, you are ready to talk yourself out of even giving entrepreneurship a chance.

Successful entrepreneurs have confronted their fears and found ways to overcome them. They have eliminated these negative blocks to unleash the power of their creativity.

The fun thing about entrepreneurship is that it is as much a process about personal growth as it is about product development and sales. Entrepreneurship is about self-actualization and reaching your full potential as a worker and a human being. It is about developing an entrepreneurial mind-set and letting go of your old corporate-driven fears. If you approach entrepreneurship in this way, it can be a self-actualizing, even spiritual, experience.

Before you launch your entrepreneurial venture, you can build your confidence by working on a business plan and developing important relationships through traditional and online networking. You will have an opportunity to do all of these things in this book.

Building Confidence in Your Business Ideas

Writing about your business ideas through blogging, tweeting, and other online methods will provide you with feedback about the positive and negative aspects of your business ideas and can help you revise your business plan. These activities allow you to test your business ideas and develop a following. Use the space provided to describe these and other actions you can take to start acting like a confident entrepreneur.

Confidence-Building Business Activity	*How It Will Help*

Creating a Support Network

It is important to talk with trusted friends and family as you think about your business idea. Who can support you during the start-up of your business? By talking to others about your plans, you become more motivated and accountable.

Success doesn't occur in a vacuum, especially for entrepreneurs. Some people will encourage and support you. With support, you will get more of what you need as you move steadily toward your destination. In some cases, you can go it alone. In other cases, you must work together with other people. Either way, without the support of others, you will be unable to maintain your motivation.

Remember that you cannot change negative people. However, they will hold you back in your attempts at self-improvement. You must learn to move from dependence to interdependence as you continue on your journey through life. Dependence means that you need others to do things for you. Interdependence means that you can get what you want by working hard, but that you also need adequate support systems to achieve your dreams. You need to share your dreams with family, friends, and colleagues. You must begin to think of yourself as part of a team. Your first assignment is to identify people in your life who can provide you with support and encouragement. These should be people to whom you can turn to make your dream become a reality—people who will encourage you if you begin to feel less motivated about achieving your dream.

Sometimes, other people feel threatened by your efforts to start and build your own business. By taking a quick inventory of your friends, neighbors, coworkers, family, and significant others, you will see that some of them are not supportive of you. Take your time and list below those people whom you feel will not be supportive of you and why you feel they will not be supportive.

Identifying Your Support Network

Person who will be supportive of me and my business (and why)

Person who will not be supportive of me and my business (and why)

You need to have a supportive network of people who can assist you. Think of your support network as a team of people dedicated to helping you achieve your goals. By discussing your goals and dreams with others, you keep the ideas alive in your mind and in your life. Others can also motivate you or keep you motivated when you find yourself getting lazy or discouraged. Your support network can help you take the necessary actions to achieve your goals. Try to get people from a variety of backgrounds to be part of your support network.

However, you must be careful whom you include in your support system. Get rid of the negative influences in your life. You cannot allow yourself to be surrounded by people who do not support you and who are not enthusiastic about seeing you achieve your dreams. There are many negative people out there who will put you down and try to convince you that you are helpless. These people should not be a part of your support system!

Instead, you need to cultivate relationships with people who will be supportive during difficult times—people you can talk to, share your feelings with, and request advice from. This support system can be critical in helping to keep you on track to achieve your dreams. People who are typically included in a support system include role models, mentors, and significant others.

Role Models

Role models are people you would like to pattern your life after. You identify with them in some way. They represent what and how you would like to be and behave. They are the standard for your ideas about success. You are probably even able to imagine yourself being like them and doing what they do. For most entrepreneurs, these behaviors include such things as perseverance, an innovative mindset, creativity, calculated risk taking, a natural curiosity, and a competitive personality. For me, author Michael E. Gerber (*Awakening the Entrepreneur Within*) has always been a role model because he has spent his life modeling many of these behaviors both in person and through his writing. He developed a formal process called the Dreaming Room in which he helps prospective entrepreneurs awaken the entrepreneurs within them. Think of people, whom you know personally or whom you may know only through what you have read about them, that you consider to be role models.

Identifying Your Role Models

Role models represent qualities or characteristics that you would like to have. Think about role models you would like to have as part of your support network. Write their names and characteristics below:

Name of Role Model	Characteristics of Role Model
_____	_____
_____	_____
_____	_____
_____	_____
_____	_____
_____	_____
_____	_____

Mentors

Most successful people, including entrepreneurs, have mentors. Mentors serve as guides, motivators, and advisors as you work to attain your dreams of starting a business. Mentors help you to grow and fulfill your potential. Now is the time to identify a mentor because this person can provide you with inspiration, information, direction, and support.

Ideally, your mentor will be someone who has started his or her own business and can guide you through the idiosyncrasies of the process because he or she has been successful. Your mentor should be someone who wants you to succeed and will take the time to help you through the beginning stages of the entrepreneurial process. You should find a mentor whom you can trust, with whom you can easily communicate, and who is interested in engaging in a mentor-mentee relationship.

Mentors can be people in your community who have experience in starting and operating their own businesses. These mentors might be entrepreneurs in traditional "bricks-and-mortar" businesses such as restaurants, bookstores, and grocery stores. On the other hand, these entrepreneurs might have experience with online or home-based businesses such as web design companies and home-based branding companies.

You also can find mentors through SCORE (Service Corps of Retired Executives) at www.score. org/mentors. SCORE mentors deliver free, confidential, and valuable advice for entrepreneurs starting their own business or those who are trying to grow an existing business. SCORE mentors can help you design and develop a business plan for your start-up or develop a marketing plan to reach customers and achieve your business goals. SCORE mentors also can assist you with financing your business idea, developing a business strategy, and developing a long-range plan for your business development and growth.

Identifying Your Mentors

Think about people who might be potential mentors to you. In the spaces below, enter their names and what they have to offer you:

Name of Mentor	*What He or She Can Offer*
_____	_____
_____	_____
_____	_____
_____	_____

Significant Others

Significant others are your closest friends and family. They are the people who are always there for you when you are starting and growing your business. They are the people with whom you share your most intimate secrets and strategies and whom you trust the most.

Some of these significant others might be people who work in your industry and can provide you with business strategies for marketing, branding, and growing your business. When I was starting my business, a friend of mine named Rick (a marketing professional) helped me to begin thinking about my business from a marketing perspective. His advice was extremely valuable in helping me to identify and market to key customers in the industry.

You may also get emotional support from significant others in your life in the form of encouragement through the ups and downs of owning your own business. My father and mother provided me with tremendous support and encouragement through the beginning stages of my business. My spouse, Kathy, now motivates me to persevere even when the economy is bad or when my business hits a snag. The following exercise will help you to think about those people in your life who have provided you with support in the past and how they can support you in your entrepreneurial venture.

Knowing How Your Significant Others Support You

In the spaces below, write the names of your closest significant others and how they support you:

Name of Significant Other	How He or She Supports Me
_____	_____
_____	_____
_____	_____
_____	_____

Getting the Support You Need

You must be open to the suggestions offered by members of your support system. You should elicit the type of support you need from each member of your support system. Examples of the types of support you might need include emotional support, practical help, advice, instruction, brainstorming, encouragement, and suggestions.

Identifying the Support You Need

List the immediate type of support you will need from people in your support system:

Name of Supporter	*What I Need from Him or Her*
_____	_____
_____	_____
_____	_____
_____	_____

Developing Ideas

The road to entrepreneurial success begins with great ideas. Most people think that great ideas come out of the blue in an "Aha!" moment in which a light bulb comes on and the entrepreneur is illuminated with a great idea for a business start-up. In most cases, it doesn't happen like that. Most often, the ideas for successful businesses begin with simple observations of your life and the lives of people around you when you say to yourself, "There has to be a better way to do this," or "How can I solve this problem more effectively?"

While on a trip to Italy, Howard Schultz, then director of marketing and operations for coffee bean retailer Starbucks, noticed that many Italians chose to buy and drink their espressos in coffee bars rather than making coffee at home. These coffee bars were inviting, community-gathering places. He thought Starbucks could grow by selling not only coffee beans but also the experience of drinking coffee in an inviting environment.

Now it's your turn! Use the worksheet that follows to explore your business ideas and how they will meet needs and solve problems in the world.

Exploring Your Ideas

In the spaces that follow, list some of your business ideas and describe how each idea will solve a problem or meet a need. Then rank your ideas from the one that interests you most (1) to the one that interests you least (4).

Entrepreneurial Idea	*Problem Solved/Need Met*
_____	_____
_____	_____
_____	_____
_____	_____

I imagine that Howard Schultz probably had doubts and fears about trying his innovative coffee shop concept, especially after the original Starbucks owners rejected his idea. You probably have doubts about your business idea, too. I certainly did. When I began developing assessments for publication, I remember people around me saying that nobody would be interested in buying something to tell them their own interests, that it would never work, and that I would be a laughingstock. If I had listened to those people and their negativity, I would have never even started as an entrepreneur. If Howard Schultz hadn't persisted by starting his own chain of coffee bars and eventually buying Starbucks, it probably would not be the international coffee phenomenon it is today.

The next step in overcoming your fears about your business ideas is to explore some of the fears and negative thoughts you are experiencing. Use the following worksheet to begin exploring your ideas and the fears associated with these ideas.

Changing Negative Thinking About Business Ideas

When you begin to have fears and negative thoughts about your business ideas, you first need to determine whether these fears are realistic. Once you have dealt with the realistic issues, you then need to restructure your thinking so that it is more positive. Think about the type of negative self-talk that tends to be present when you think about your business ideas. Then list some of the positive talk you can change it to.

Negative thinking usually takes one of three forms: worrier, perfectionist, or critic. Worriers say "What if...?"

"What if nobody buys my product or service?"

"What if the economy gets worse?"

"What if I can't fill all my orders?"

List some things you say to yourself when you are worrying about your business ideas:

_____

_____

_____

_____

Try to change these "what if" statements to positive statements about possibilities. For example, you can change "What if nobody buys my product or service?" to "I will make it or offer it, and I'm sure people will buy it." You can change the thought "What if the economy gets worse?" to "I can't control what happens economically, but I can control how I market my product." Lastly, you can reword the worry "What if I can't fill all my orders?" to "Having too many orders to fill is a great problem. I will hire more people if I need to."

Turn the worries you listed into positive statements:

_____

_____

_____

_____

Perfectionists say "I must . . ." and "I should have. . . ."

"I must have the perfect product!"

"I should have started when I was younger!"

"I should have found a way to get financing."

List some perfectionistic things you say to yourself about your business:

_____

_____

_____

(continued)

Changing Negative Thinking About Business Ideas (continued)

Nobody is perfect, so it makes sense to reframe these types of statements in a more realistic and positive way. For example, you can change "I must have the perfect product!" to "I will develop the best product I can, and people will buy it." "I should have started when I was younger!" can be changed to "I now have more experience to be successful in my entrepreneurial venture!" And "I should have found a way to get financing" can be changed to "It is never too late for me to get financing for my start-up."

Now it's your turn to change the perfectionistic things you say to yourself into realistic, positive statements:

_____

_____

_____

_____

Critics say "I can't . . ." or "I'm not. . . ."

"I can't do my own marketing."

"I can't start my own business without experience."

"I'm not a salesperson."

List some critical things you say to yourself about your business ideas:

_____

_____

_____

_____

Even criticism can be changed into a positive statement. "I can't do my own marketing" can be changed to "I will learn as much as I can about marketing, and I will also consult professionals at SCORE for more help in marketing my product." "I can't start my own business without experience" can be changed to "I am as smart and persistent as others who have started their own businesses." "I'm not a salesperson" can be changed to "I'm not great at sales yet, but I'm working on overcoming my fears of networking and promoting my product."

Use the space below to change the criticisms you listed into positive statements:

_____

_____

_____

_____

_____

_____

Another method for overcoming your fears about your business ideas is to talk to others about your ideas. I know that you have not yet narrowed down your options for starting a business, and you will have the opportunity to develop business ideas later on. However, at this juncture, you may find it helpful to begin talking about your business ideas with significant others in your life.

Gathering Feedback on Your Ideas

In the table that follows, list the people whom you have talked to about your start-up ideas and how they reacted and the suggestions they made.

Person	Reactions	Suggestions
_____	_____	_____
_____	_____	_____
_____	_____	_____
_____	_____	_____
_____	_____	_____

Not everyone is going to like your business ideas. You need to be prepared for a certain amount of rejection and ridicule. When I first started my business, I was rejected by more than 10 publishing companies before one was willing to publish my materials. So although it is important to listen to the opinions of others and integrate any suggestions that you feel are constructive, do not let others talk you out of a business idea that you think will be lucrative.

Facing Fears About Job Security

The thought of quitting your job to start a business and then having your business fail is a legitimate concern. Remember that fears related to job security are normal and experienced in one form or another by all entrepreneurs. There are several ways that you can handle these fears about job security:

- Reduce your spending so that you will have more money for your business start-up.

- Begin your entrepreneurial venture on the side while maintaining a full-time corporate job. In this way, if the business does not do as well as projected, you still have a full-time job for your finances.

- Leave your full-time corporate job for a part-time job that would take up less of your time, thus freeing up more time to work on your business.

- Examine the risk-reward ratio of starting your own business. Risk-reward ratios are most often calculated by investors to compare the expected returns of an investment to the amount of risk undertaken to attain these returns. You can do the same thing for quitting a corporate job to start your own business by calculating the amount of profit you expect to make in your business as compared to the amount you will lose if your business fails.

Answer the questions in the following worksheet to address how you will confront fears regarding job security.

Overcoming Fears About Job Security

Explore your job security fears and come up with actions you can take to resolve them by responding to the following questions:

How can you reduce your spending?

_____

_____

How can you approach your business start-up so that you can maintain your full-time job?

_____

_____

What type of part-time position could you search for and get to provide you with more time for your start-up?

_____

_____

What do you think is the greatest risk of leaving a full-time job?

_____

_____

What do you think would be the greatest reward of leaving a full-time job?

_____

_____

Handling Your Finances

If you are planning to cut your hours or leave the security of your job, you need to make sure that you have a financial cushion to help you land on your feet or have investors to help you get through the lean start-up months. The cost of starting your own business may not be as expensive as you think it will be, but it may require you and your family to rethink how you spend your money.

The start-up costs of any business can be expensive, so the more money you have saved the greater your peace of mind will be. Once your business gets off the ground, you will have control over your finances. Until you reach that point, however, you'll do well to have some capital saved for emergencies.

People planning to quit their jobs to launch a full-time business need three to six months of expenses saved. This "bootstrapping" money (money set aside from your savings, your salary, or profits from selling assets) will provide you with income during the lean start-up period.

Thus, if your monthly family income is $2,000, you will need to set aside somewhere between $6,000 and $12,000. Saving this much money before you quit your job or reduce your hours will help you feel good about your transition from corporate life to entrepreneurship.

Tracking Your Savings

Your monthly income: $ _____

Six months of your family income: $ _____

Amount saved so far: $ _____

Amount still needed: $ _____

How long do you think it will take to save this money? _____

Achieving Balance

For you to be happy and successful in your own business, you need to be able to balance work, leisure, and your family life. In fact, for many people, leisure and family are the antidote to the stress of starting and owning their own business.

Assessing Your Work–Leisure Balance

Ultimately, the relationship between your work and leisure life, and the effects of the balance (or imbalance) between the two, can take a variety of forms:

- **Separation:** Your business and leisure are two distinct facets of your life that do not influence each other. Although this is possible, it is hard to imagine that the time put into your business and the money earned from it have no impact on your hobbies or interests, or that leisure activities have no effect on your business life. True separation may be quite difficult to manage.

  List those times when your business and leisure activities are separated from each other:

  _____

  _____

  _____

  _____

- **Spillover:** There is little or no distinction between your business and your leisure. You find so much satisfaction engaging in one activity that you choose to do it in both your work and leisure time. Imagine someone who owns a dog-walking business who spends her time volunteering in an animal shelter.

  List those times when your business and leisure activities spill over into each other:

  _____

  _____

  _____

  _____

  _____

- **Compensation:** What may be lacking in one arena of life can be compensated for by satisfying activities in another, as in the case of a business owner whose life is enhanced by family vacations and activities.

  List those times when your business and leisure activities compensate for each other:

  _____

  _____

  _____

  _____

- **Conflict:** High levels of demand in one area of life can cause conflicts in the other. Such conflicts are frequent and are often part of the career management process, although they can be avoided and managed. A person who is working too much at his or her business may experience difficulties at home with family members—a common complaint among workers who feel the pressure to put their careers first.

  List those times when your business and leisure activities conflict with each other:

  _____

  _____

  _____

  _____

Recognize the patterns that your work and leisure take and how they interact with each other. Identifying the effects that interaction has on your well-being is key to maintaining a successful business.

In addition to simply choosing and engaging in your favorite leisure activities, consider the following as you seek to find your balance:

- **Time for relationships:** Take time each day to connect with important people in your life. This may mean scheduling this time (actually writing it in a calendar or planner) until you begin to adopt it as a permanent part of your day.

- **Time alone:** Take time for yourself. Use it to reflect and recharge. If you know how, try meditating for an hour a day. Meditation can help you focus on the moment and stop thinking about work that needs to be done in the future.

- **Breaks:** You can easily build breaks into your work schedule. Even if you have been working quite well without taking breaks, you probably have not experienced your optimum level of creativity, motivation, and energy. Almost all employers allow for some breaks during the day.

- **Exercise:** Exercise has been shown to be an excellent stress buster. People who exercise regularly tend to be happier and more energetic and have a better outlook on life. They are able to cope much more effectively with stress.

- **Vacations:** Use your vacation time for rest and relaxation. Of course, everyone has a different idea about what constitutes rest and relaxation. My wife and I love international vacations with lots of sightseeing. Our neighbors prefer to rent a cabin on the lake only an hour out of town. The secret is to commit to using your vacation days (don't try to carry them over without a great reason for doing so) and finding a restful way to spend them.

Chapter 2 helped you address the fears that are associated with leaving a secure corporate job to start your own business. Every entrepreneur who has made this leap will tell you that you are not alone and that it is a scary, risky proposition. However, each of these entrepreneurs would also tell you that owning and operating his or her own business was one of the most rewarding experiences of his or her career and life. Chapter 3 helps you discover the type of entrepreneur you are.

Part 2: Generating Business Ideas

"The entrepreneur in us sees opportunities everywhere we look, but many people see only problems everywhere they look. The entrepreneur in us is more concerned with discriminating between opportunities than he or she is with failing to see the opportunities."

—Michael Gerber

Identify the Best Business Type for You

Before any entrepreneurial venture begins, there is an idea. Entrepreneurs live in a world where ideas can be built, created, and transformed into a reality-based, money-making machine. Henry Ford, the founder of the Ford Motor Company, had an idea about a car that could be mass produced easily and affordably; Steve Jobs, the founder of Apple, had an idea about a computer that anyone could afford and use; and Ray Kroc, the founder of McDonald's, had an idea about producing a fast-food hamburger that was as good or better than one you could make at home.

Generating business ideas is not easy. Identifying a business idea that will be viable for you requires a great deal of creative thinking. You must be willing to allow yourself to "think outside of the occupational box" in order to stimulate your creative problem solving.

Because all new entrepreneurial ventures involve trying novel ideas, the objective at this stage is to generate business ideas that you may not have considered before. You need to dig down deep and think beyond the most obvious choices. For instance, you may have a job as an accountant, so the first thing that comes to mind may have something to do with accounting or auditing. However, you also may have volunteered with the local animal shelter, and thus might generate business ideas such as pet groomer and dog walker. For me, the most obvious choice was to open a private counseling practice. If I chose not to dig any deeper than that, I may have missed out on a skill—writing—that I had not used since high school and college.

Because there are thousands of different types of businesses to begin, you need a systematic way to find the right business opportunities for you. Generating business ideas related to your interests, skills, and personality can be a difficult but necessary piece of the entrepreneurial puzzle. You will need a proven process for becoming alert to the many opportunities that match your personal characteristics.

One way to focus your thinking about potential business ideas is to consider your type. In general, your type is the combination of your personal preferences, attitudes, and abilities. Your entrepreneurial type is these aspects of your genetic makeup as they relate to starting a business. The different methodologies entrepreneurs use to implement their business ideas are loosely based on their individual types. By understanding what type of entrepreneur you are, you have a much greater chance of identifying a business format in which you can easily succeed.

The Five Forms of Entrepreneurship

In the 1930s, the father of modern entrepreneurship, Joseph A. Schumpeter, proposed that entrepreneurship and innovation were intricately intertwined. He felt that innovation and entrepreneurship took five primary forms:

- A new product or new quality of a product
- A new product founded upon scientific discovery
- The opening of a brand-new market
- A new source of raw materials
- A new service

The Entrepreneurial Type Scale

The Entrepreneurial Type Scale (ETS) can help you identify the specific type of entrepreneur you are. This assessment will allow you to explore the various ways that entrepreneurs implement their business ideas and to identify the one that best suits you.

This assessment contains 60 statements. Read each of the statements and decide whether the statement is true or false. If it is true, circle the word *True* next to the statement. If the statement is false, circle the word *False* next to the statement. Do not spend too much time thinking about your answers, and don't worry about totaling your answers at this point. Be sure to respond to every statement.

Product

1.	I am imaginative.	True	False
2.	I am very creative.	True	False
3.	I would rather create products than sell them.	True	False
4.	I'm more satisfied creating something for myself.	True	False
5.	I like working on projects independently.	True	False
6.	I am artistic.	True	False

Create It Total: _____

7.	I'm comfortable making "cold calls" to sell things.	True	False
8.	I could easily sell something to a stranger.	True	False
9.	I like to/would like to go out and get customers.	True	False
10.	I'm likely to measure success by the sales I make.	True	False
11.	I don't let rejection get me down.	True	False
12.	People say I could sell anything.	True	False

Sell It Total: _____

13.	I like assembling things.	True	False
14.	I like to fix things.	True	False
15.	I am good at working with my hands.	True	False
16.	I am a natural-born builder.	True	False
17.	I like using hand tools.	True	False
18.	I can make a product to sell.	True	False

Repair or Build It Total: _____

19.	I like to read and write.	True	False
20.	I am a creative writer.	True	False
21.	I can persuade people with my writing.	True	False
22.	I enjoy doing research and writing about what I learned.	True	False
23.	I can write materials to promote the sale of products.	True	False
24.	I express myself well through writing.	True	False

Write About It Total: _____

25.	I'm taking a big financial risk in starting a business.	True	False
26.	I worry about the legal problems that accompany a new business.	True	False
27.	I'm convinced I could make a lot of money in my own business.	True	False
28.	I'm willing to start my business in my spare time to save money.	True	False

(continued)

(continued)

29. People often come to me for help with their computers.	True	False
30. I'm good at understanding how technology works.	True	False

Understand It Total: _____

Service

31. I try to understand human nature.	True	False
32. I like to help others be successful.	True	False
33. People come to me for advice.	True	False
34. I am good at solving problems.	True	False
35. I enjoy showing others how to achieve their goals.	True	False
36. I like to work one-on-one.	True	False

Consult About It Total: _____

37. I am good at arranging things.	True	False
38. I am highly detail oriented.	True	False
39. I am fascinated with how organizations work.	True	False
40. People say I'm organized.	True	False
41. I'm better at numbers than words.	True	False
42. I'm usually the one who coordinates things.	True	False

Organize It Total: _____

43. I'm a very nurturing person.	True	False
44. I would like to help someone recover from an injury.	True	False
45. I would like caring for a sick person.	True	False
46. I like to care for homeless animals.	True	False
47. People come to me for help.	True	False
48. People say I am caring and kind.	True	False

Care for It Total: _____

49. I like to make people feel welcome.	True	False
50. I like to network.	True	False
51. I am a social person.	True	False
52. I'm better with words than numbers.	True	False
53. People say I am a great speaker.	True	False
54. I am outgoing.	True	False

Entertain It Total: _____

55. I am a good teacher.	True	False
56. I can help people understand difficult concepts.	True	False
57. I like to help people learn new things.	True	False
58. I can explain things well to others.	True	False
59. I can train others to improve their skills.	True	False
60. I can teach any subject/topic.	True	False
Teach It Total: _____		

Scoring

The Entrepreneurial Type Scale is designed to help you to identify the best way for you to implement your business idea. The ETS will help you in understanding the type of entrepreneur you are and which types of businesses you might want to pursue and those you might want to avoid. To score the ETS, you need to first determine your scores on each of the individual scales for both the products and services groupings.

To score the ETS, look at the 60 items you just completed. For each scale, simply count the number of True responses you circled in each section. Put that number in the space marked "Total" at the end of each section. Use the spaces below to transfer your scores for each of the scales. Then add your individual scores together to get your overall totals for the Product and Service columns.

Create It Total: _____   Consult About It Total: _____

Sell It Total: _____   Organize It Total: _____

Repair or Build It Total: _____   Care for It Total: _____

Write About It Total: _____   Entertain It Total: _____

Understand It Total: _____   Teach It Total: _____

Product Grand Total: _____   **Service Grand Total:** _____

Scores from 0 to 1 on the individual scales are low and indicate that this method is not a good fit for your entrepreneurial type and that you are not well suited to implement your business idea in this manner.

Scores from 2 to 4 on the individual scales are average and indicate that this method may potentially be a good fit for your entrepreneurial type and that you are somewhat suited to implement your business idea in this manner.

Scores from 5 to 6 on the individual scales are high and indicate that this method is a very good fit for your entrepreneurial type and that you are very well suited to implement your business idea in this manner.

Regardless of your scores on the assessment, you should complete all of the sections that follow. The higher your scores on an individual scale of the assessment, the better suited you are to implement your business idea using that methodology.

Primary Entrepreneurial Types

As an entrepreneur, there are a variety of businesses you can start, but they all belong to one of the two major business categories: product and service. Look back to your grand totals for each of these two categories. The higher your score, the more effective you will be in launching that type of business.

- **Product:** In this type of business, you make and sell products to others for a profit. These types of businesses are often started as an outgrowth of a hobby or leisure activity. They often begin with an idea for a product that is not readily available on the market. For these types of businesses, it is important to have a clearly defined market and the ability to produce the product(s) in a cost-effective manner. These products can be such things as toys, paintings, mailboxes, pottery, dolls, and much more.

- **Service:** Service businesses are ones in which you perform a personal service for people for a fee. The service may be performed for another business or for an individual customer. The service is usually something that customers cannot do or prefer not to do themselves. Examples of such services include repairing lawn mowers, painting houses, counseling, providing child care, recruiting employees, accounting, house cleaning, blacktopping driveways, pet sitting, and landscaping.

The following sections detail the five entrepreneurial types within these two primary business categories.

Product-Oriented Entrepreneurs

Product-oriented entrepreneurs are best suited to begin businesses in which they are creating products to sell. For each of the five product-oriented entrepreneurial types, complete the journaling activities that follow the type descriptions. You should begin with those areas in which you scored highest on the ETS.

Create It

Many entrepreneurs are very creative and innovative in the businesses they begin. Entrepreneurs who are skilled at creating include artists, craftspeople, designers, innovators, and developers. They are able to work with available materials to make a new product to sell to their customers. They are good at producing products that people need and are willing to pay for.

Exploring Your Creativity

1. What do you like to create?

_____

_____

2. What is your best skill or talent related to creating products?

_____

_____

3. What is your vision of a product for the marketplace?

_____

_____

Sell It

Many entrepreneurs operate businesses in which they sell products that they make or ones that they purchase from other people or other businesses. They tend to be self-directed, persistent, people-oriented, and assertive in selling their products. They may sell either directly to consumers or to other businesses. Entrepreneurs who are skilled at sales include real estate agents, cosmetics salespeople, insurance salespeople, and auto salespeople.

Evaluating Your Sales Skills

1. What are your greatest people skills?

_____

_____

2. What would you be proficient in selling?

_____

_____

(continued)

Evaluating Your Sales Skills (continued)

3. How do you deal with rejection when you are selling?

_____

_____

Repair or Build It

Many entrepreneurs enjoy working with their hands doing some sort of manual labor work such as repairing computers, carpentry, or laying tile. They enjoy repairing things or building something from scratch and are good at what are considered the trades or skilled trades. They are driven to build something tangible where nothing exists or repair things to make them run more efficiently or smoothly.

Working with Your Hands

1. What are your best manual skills?

_____

_____

2. What could you build that people would buy?

_____

_____

3. What could you repair that people would pay for?

_____

_____

Write About It

Many entrepreneurs use their ability to communicate in their business. For people who can communicate clearly in writing, there are many options. They communicate in print media through magazine articles, books, technical writing, newspapers, newsletters, and marketing materials. They also communicate through screenplays, presentations, blogs, and websites.

Recognizing the Writer in You

1. What types of things do you write?

_____

_____

2. Who is your primary audience?

_____

_____

3. What murky subjects do you bring clarity to in your writing?

_____

_____

Understand It

Many entrepreneurs are happiest in businesses in which they are trying to understand and figure things out. They are curious and want to learn how things work. They enjoy tinkering with new technology and playing with new equipment. They want to start a business that involves technology. They are patient in studying and learning about how new technologies work.

Learning About Your Technical Skills

1. What types of technology do you work best with?

_____

_____

2. What types of technical problems can you solve for people?

_____

_____

(continued)

Learning About Your Technical Skills (continued)

3. What technical subject are you most curious about?

_____

_____

Service-Oriented Entrepreneurs

Service-oriented entrepreneurs are best suited to begin businesses in which they are providing a specific service to others. For each of the five service-oriented entrepreneurial types, complete the journaling activities that follow the type descriptions. You should begin with those areas in which you scored highest on the ETS.

Consult About It

Entrepreneurs in almost any area of specialization can build a consulting business. Consultants are brought into a business to solve a specific problem. Businesses usually will hire a consultant when they need a specialist in an area they are not familiar with. Consultants charge businesses (or individuals) to provide solid and logical advice. Most consultants specialize in a narrowly focused field.

Finding Your Specialty

1. What do you consider your area of specialization?

_____

_____

2. What types of problems can you solve for people?

_____

_____

3. How can you improve an existing system?

_____

_____

Organize It

Increased outsourcing has increased opportunity for entrepreneurs with strong organizational skills. These entrepreneurs are proficient at businesses in which they are organizing systems or people. They tend to be good at working with numbers and coordinating human and physical resources. Attentive to details and reliable for meeting deadlines, they also are good at helping people put their personal and professional lives in order.

Being Organized

1. What types of things or people do you organize best?

_____

_____

2. What numerical programs (such as Excel and SPSS) do you excel at?

_____

_____

3. What critical business functions (such as accounting, budgeting, and financial analysis) do you excel at?

_____

_____

Care for It

There is a great need for entrepreneurs interested in caring for other people, animals, things, plants, and the earth. Such people are interested in providing ongoing care, assistance, and counseling to help make the world a better place in which to live. They are nurturing, supportive, caring, and helpful. Many of these types of entrepreneurs are interested in finding ways to help people who need to be cared for.

Caring for Customers

1. What helping expertise do you have that people will pay for?

_____

_____

2. What types of people would you like to care for?

_____

_____

3. What types of things, plants, or animals would you like to care for?

_____

_____

Entertain It

Entertaining entrepreneurs prefer to work with people than with things or data. They enjoy interacting with people, making them feel welcome and happy and ensuring that they have a good time. These entrepreneurs thrive in hospitality-related businesses such as restaurants, bars, and coffeehouses. They also succeed in the entertainment industry and service businesses such as spas.

Finding Your Entertainment Value

1. What types of people would you like to entertain?

_____

_____

2. How would you entertain them?

_____

_____

3. How do you interact best with people?

_____

_____

_____

Teach It

Many people start their own business in which they can use their training and teaching skills to help others learn new skills or improve existing skills. These entrepreneurs usually specialize in specific topics such as time management or social skills, while others are generalists. Some of these entrepreneurs develop their own curriculum to teach while others who are skilled teachers or trainers will teach pre-existing programs developed by someone else.

Trying Teaching

1. What could you teach others in your business?

_____

_____

2. Who could you teach in your business?

_____

_____

3. Where could you teach others in your business?

_____

_____

One of the most important aspects of starting your own business is being able to generate business ideas and then make those ideas a reality. The first step in generating business ideas is to identify your entrepreneurial type or best method for making your idea a reality. Use what you have learned about entrepreneurial types in this chapter to complete the following worksheet.

Identifying Your Top Three Entrepreneurial Types

Review your ETS results. Based on your scores and the worksheets you have completed, are you more suited to a product business or a service business?

_____

Look back in the "Scoring" section at the five entrepreneurial types in the category listed above. Which of these did you score the highest in? Then think about which worksheets in this chapter were easiest for you to complete. Use the following space to list the three entrepreneurial types you are most excited about and have the most ideas for. This list will help you to generate business ideas that will work best for you.

_____

_____

_____

This chapter has helped you to explore the various ways that you might begin generating business ideas. This chapter will serve as a templte that you will use again in Chapter 4 and Chapter 5. Chapter 4 will help you begin to think about your passions and how those passions might be potential businesses that you can begin.

Find Your Passion

Entrepreneurship is a roller-coaster ride that can be both scary and exciting. The people who remain motivated through the rough times are those entrepreneurs who are extremely passionate about their product or service. Those businesses that tend to fail within the first year or so often do so because the owner is not passionate about the product or service being marketed.

As an entrepreneur, you need to be intricately aware of your specific interests before you begin to organize your business ideas and think about implementing a business. By identifying the areas of work in which you are most interested, you will always be safe with the knowledge that you love your product or service. If you are promoting something you truly feel excited about, others will get excited, too. In this chapter, you will explore those things you enjoy doing and start to figure out a way to build your business around these interests.

Understanding What Interest Inventories Do

Interest inventories have been around for centuries and have been used to help people reflect on their lives in order to identify prominent interests that they have engaged in on an ongoing basis. By using an interest inventory, people uncover many more interests than if they simply responded to a question about what they enjoy.

You can use the Entrepreneurial Interest Inventory in this chapter to reflect on aspects of your-self that you might not have thought about for a long time. You will remember interests that you might have pursued in the past and forgot. There may even be some interests that you have not pursued since you were a child. You probably also have interests that you never thought about in relation to a business venture. It does not matter whether you pursue these interests in your work, leisure-time activities, or time with family and friends. Now is the time for you to think about all of the activities that have held your interest in the past or might hold your interest in the future.

The Entrepreneurial Interest Inventory can be tremendously beneficial to your thinking about the type of business you would like to own and operate by helping you to

- Clarify your true interests, not those activities that other people believe you should engage in.
- Translate those interests into various types of business ideas.
- Organize your interests in a meaningful, structured way.
- Stimulate the exploration and identification of various business ideas.
- Provide insight into business options you do not want to pursue.
- Verify that your business ideas are related to your true interests.
- Reassure you if you already know your interests.
- Generate multiple business ideas related to your strongest interests.

Of course, the last one is the ultimate goal of this chapter and one of the main goals of this book. Remember that the more you know about yourself, the better your odds of achieving success in owning and operating a business.

Ask Friends and Family

Rhonda Abrams, author of the best-selling book *What Business Should I Start?* (Planning Shop, 2004), suggests another method for identifying your entrepreneurial interests. She says that you almost certainly have many more interests than those that will immediately pop into your mind. She suggests that you take this opportunity to talk with people whom you know well. Ask these people to share their insights about you. Abrams contends that people who have known you for a long time may remember some of the interests that you have forgotten about. What would your friends and family members say are your greatest interests?

The Entrepreneurial Interest Inventory

The Entrepreneurial Interest Inventory is designed to help you explore business ideas based on your interests. Read each of the items, decide how much you would enjoy engaging in that activity, and circle the appropriate response using the following scale:

> 4 = Very Interested
>
> 3 = Somewhat Interested
>
> 2 = A Little Interested
>
> 1 = Not Interested

This is not a test. There are no right or wrong answers, so do not spend too much time thinking about your responses. Be sure to respond to every statement. Do not worry about totaling your scores at this point.

How interested are you in . . .	Very Interested	Somewhat Interested	A Little Interested	Not Interested
1. Planting and trimming trees?	4	3	2	1
2. Managing and protecting natural resources?	4	3	2	1
3. Caring for animals?	4	3	2	1
4. Applying technology to farming?	4	3	2	1
5. Studying the composition of soil?	4	3	2	1
6. Experimenting with plants?	4	3	2	1

Section 1 Total: _____

How interested are you in . . .	Very Interested	Somewhat Interested	A Little Interested	Not Interested
7. Crafting products from wood?	4	3	2	1
8. Operating heavy equipment?	4	3	2	1
9. Working with tools?	4	3	2	1
10. Using computers to prepare detailed drawings?	4	3	2	1
11. Planning, designing, and directing construction projects?	4	3	2	1
12. Creating safe and functional buildings?	4	3	2	1

Section 2 Total: _____

How interested are you in . . .	Very Interested	Somewhat Interested	A Little Interested	Not Interested
13. Researching and writing news stories?	4	3	2	1
14. Singing in a professional choir?	4	3	2	1

(continued)

(continued)

How interested are you in . . .	Very Interested	Somewhat Interested	A Little Interested	Not Interested
15. Preparing public relations information?	4	3	2	1
16. Painting or sketching landscapes or portraits?	4	3	2	1
17. Doing commercial art or design projects?	4	3	2	1
18. Dancing in a variety show or acting in a play?	4	3	2	1

Section 3 Total: _____

How interested are you in . . .	Very Interested	Somewhat Interested	A Little Interested	Not Interested
19. Providing feedback to and motivating others?	4	3	2	1
20. Analyzing numerical information?	4	3	2	1
21. Leading people?	4	3	2	1
22. Calculating expenses and profits?	4	3	2	1
23. Managing a department or an organization?	4	3	2	1
24. Handling tax issues for companies or individuals?	4	3	2	1

Section 4 Total: _____

How interested are you in . . .	Very Interested	Somewhat Interested	A Little Interested	Not Interested
25. Teaching reading, English, or math?	4	3	2	1
26. Watching children at a day-care center?	4	3	2	1
27. Managing education programs?	4	3	2	1
28. Working with special-needs students?	4	3	2	1
29. Teaching life skills to adults?	4	3	2	1
30. Tutoring students who are having trouble in school?	4	3	2	1

Section 5 Total: _____

How interested are you in . . .	Very Interested	Somewhat Interested	A Little Interested	Not Interested
31. Analyzing and tracking investments?	4	3	2	1
32. Preparing financial reports?	4	3	2	1
33. Buying and selling stocks and bonds?	4	3	2	1
34. Studying financial trends?	4	3	2	1
35. Selling insurance policies?	4	3	2	1
36. Helping people plan their retirement?	4	3	2	1

Section 6 Total: _____

How interested are you in . . .	Very Interested	Somewhat Interested	A Little Interested	Not Interested
37. Examining financial documents for errors?	4	3	2	1
38. Planning land use in cities?	4	3	2	1
39. Inspecting damage from and preventing forest fires?	4	3	2	1
40. Keeping accounting records for a government agency?	4	3	2	1
41. Researching crime?	4	3	2	1
42. Analyzing and managing information about the earth?	4	3	2	1

Section 7 Total: _____

How interested are you in . . .	Very Interested	Somewhat Interested	A Little Interested	Not Interested
43. Diagnosing and treating illnesses?	4	3	2	1
44. Helping people with physical and emotional needs?	4	3	2	1
45. Working as an aide in a hospital?	4	3	2	1
46. Rescuing people in emergency situations?	4	3	2	1
47. Helping people maintain healthy teeth?	4	3	2	1
48. Researching diseases and cures?	4	3	2	1

Section 8 Total: _____

How interested are you in . . .	Very Interested	Somewhat Interested	A Little Interested	Not Interested
49. Preparing and/or serving meals for others?	4	3	2	1
50. Cutting and styling hair?	4	3	2	1
51. Guiding groups through the outdoors?	4	3	2	1
52. Teaching tourists how to do an outdoor activity?	4	3	2	1
53. Helping people plan trips?	4	3	2	1
54. Managing a hotel or motel?	4	3	2	1

Section 9 Total: _____

How interested are you in . . .	Very Interested	Somewhat Interested	A Little Interested	Not Interested
55. Helping students manage stress effectively?	4	3	2	1
56. Working in a mental health clinic?	4	3	2	1
57. Helping people in crises?	4	3	2	1
58. Providing marriage counseling?	4	3	2	1
59. Doing social service work?	4	3	2	1
60. Working with juveniles on probation?	4	3	2	1

Section 10 Total: _____

(continued)

(continued)

How interested are you in . . .	Very Interested	Somewhat Interested	A Little Interested	Not Interested
61. Repairing computers?	4	3	2	1
62. Assisting people in using technology?	4	3	2	1
63. Managing an organization's network?	4	3	2	1
64. Writing computer programs and software?	4	3	2	1
65. Setting up or managing websites?	4	3	2	1
66. Finding new ways to prevent computer viruses?	4	3	2	1

Section 11 Total: _____

How interested are you in . . .	Very Interested	Somewhat Interested	A Little Interested	Not Interested
67. Helping people solve legal problems?	4	3	2	1
68. Using equipment to fight fires?	4	3	2	1
69. Collecting evidence to solve a criminal case?	4	3	2	1
70. Enforcing laws and regulations?	4	3	2	1
71. Preparing and arguing legal cases for trial?	4	3	2	1
72. Protecting people and property from harm?	4	3	2	1

Section 12 Total: _____

How interested are you in . . .	Very Interested	Somewhat Interested	A Little Interested	Not Interested
73. Setting up machines according to written standards?	4	3	2	1
74. Producing precision metal and wood products?	4	3	2	1
75. Operating lathes and drill presses?	4	3	2	1
76. Disassembling and repairing machinery?	4	3	2	1
77. Repairing televisions and other electronic devices?	4	3	2	1
78. Inspecting and evaluating the quality of products?	4	3	2	1

Section 13 Total: _____

How interested are you in . . .	Very Interested	Somewhat Interested	A Little Interested	Not Interested
79. Planning advertising campaigns?	4	3	2	1
80. Raising funds for an organization?	4	3	2	1
81. Persuading others to buy something?	4	3	2	1
82. Selling products over the Internet?	4	3	2	1
83. Helping people buy and sell homes?	4	3	2	1
84. Explaining and demonstrating the use of products?	4	3	2	1

Section 14 Total: _____

How interested are you in . . .	Very Interested	Somewhat Interested	A Little Interested	Not Interested
85. Solving difficult math problems?	4	3	2	1
86. Conducting chemistry experiments?	4	3	2	1
87. Collecting and analyzing natural objects?	4	3	2	1
88. Studying the nature of the universe?	4	3	2	1
89. Researching and developing products for a corporation?	4	3	2	1
90. Constructing and interpreting maps, graphs, and diagrams?	4	3	2	1
Section 15 Total: _____				

How interested are you in . . .	Very Interested	Somewhat Interested	A Little Interested	Not Interested
91. Maintaining automobile engines?	4	3	2	1
92. Driving a truck or taxi cab?	4	3	2	1
93. Driving a bus from city to city?	4	3	2	1
94. Doing auto body repairs?	4	3	2	1
95. Flying airplanes and helicopters?	4	3	2	1
96. Transporting passengers and cargo?	4	3	2	1
Section 16 Total: _____				

Scoring

For each of the 16 sections on the previous pages, add the numbers you circled for each item. Put that total on the line at the end of each section. The higher the total number for each section, the more important it is for you to pursue those types of interests when you are making career decisions:

- A score from 6 to 12 indicates a low level of interest
- A score from 13 to 18 indicates an average level of interest
- A score from 19 to 24 indicates a high level of interest

Your results will help you focus your exploration of potential businesses by revealing your strongest interests.

Matching Your Interests to Business Idea Categories

Information about entrepreneurial interests can be organized by using career clusters. The Entrepreneurial Interest Inventory is made up of 16 sections representing the United States Department of Education's 16 major career clusters. Those clusters, in turn, represent the majority of available business options.

For each of the 16 areas that follow, list your score from that section of the Entrepreneurial Interest Inventory and whether it was low, average, or high.

1. **Agriculture and Natural Resources:** An interest in working with plants, animals, forests, or mineral resources for agriculture, horticulture, conservation, and other purposes.

   Interest: _____

2. **Architecture and Construction:** An interest in designing, assembling, and maintaining buildings and other structures.

   Interest: _____

3. **Arts and Communication:** An interest in creatively expressing feelings or ideas, communicating news or information, or performing.

   Interest: _____

4. **Business and Administration:** An interest in making an organization run smoothly.

   Interest: _____

5. **Education and Training:** An interest in helping people learn.

   Interest: _____

6. **Finance and Insurance:** An interest in helping businesses and people secure their financial future.

   Interest: _____

7. **Government and Public Administration:** An interest in helping a government agency serve the needs of the public.

   Interest: _____

8. **Health Science:** An interest in helping people and animals be healthy.

   Interest: _____

9. **Hospitality, Tourism, and Recreation:** An interest in catering to the wishes and needs of others so they may enjoy a clean environment, good food and drink, comfortable accommodations, and recreation.

   Interest: _____

10. **Human Service:** An interest in improving people's social, mental, emotional, or spiritual well-being.

    Interest: _____

11. **Information Technology:** An interest in designing, developing, managing, and supporting information systems.

    Interest: _____

12. **Law and Public Safety:** An interest in upholding people's rights or in protecting people and property.

    Interest: _____

13. **Manufacturing:** An interest in processing materials into products or maintaining and repairing products by using machines or hand tools.

    Interest: _____

14. **Retail and Wholesale Sales and Service:** An interest in bringing others to a particular point of view through personal persuasion and sales techniques.

    Interest: _____

15. **Scientific Research, Engineering, and Mathematics:** An interest in discovering, collecting, and analyzing information about the natural world, life sciences, and human behavior.

    Interest: _____

16. **Transportation, Distribution, and Logistics:** An interest in operations that move people or materials.

    Interest: _____

Finding Your Top Three Career Clusters of Interest

Looking back over your results, which of the 16 career clusters yielded the highest total score? Use the following space to list the three career clusters you scored highest in. This list provides an excellent clue as to the kind of business you will find the most satisfaction in (and will probably market the best).

1. _____

2. _____

3. _____

Generating Business Ideas Based on Your Interests

Opportunity recognition refers to the process entrepreneurs use to identify problems to solve or needs to be fulfilled, and then creating a business idea to do so. Most theories of opportunity recognition describe it as a process that combines creativity and factual information. This process begins in two stages:

- **Preparation.** In this stage, you explore your experience and knowledge to identify your basic interests for entrepreneurship. This exploration usually starts from a conscious self-reflection of your interests (this chapter) and skills (the next chapter).

- **Incubation.** In this stage, you begin to think about a problem or idea you could base your business around. You will benefit most by taking the information in the preparation stage and using it to begin considering possibilities and options. The incubation stage is best completed by intermingling ideas in a fairly structured manner and searching for all possible options.

Some people have ideas pop into their heads all the time. Others need to go through a process of discovery. If you are one of the lucky people who see opportunities everywhere and are able to quickly and easily generate business ideas, the following worksheet will help you to organize your thoughts. If you have to process information more thoroughly and reflect on the needs of society, refer to the following questions to help you generate business ideas and complete the worksheet. Answer these questions based on your primary interests and entrepreneurial type (which you identified in Chapter 3):

- What product or service is needed?
- What would make life easier?
- What would make things more convenient?
- What would provide people with a better life?
- What are people complaining about?
- What could be done more easily?
- What could be provided at a lower cost?
- What are the current trends?
- What could you use in your community?
- What is needed in this economy?

If these questions do not help you to generate ideas for your business, look at the appendix for ideas related to your interests.

Incubating Your Interests

At the top of each of the tables that follow, list your highest interest areas (Health Science, Information Technology, and so on) from the Entrepreneurial Interests Inventory you completed in this chapter. In the left-hand column of each table, write your top entrepreneurial types from Chapter 3. Then, in the right-hand column, list all of the potential entrepreneurial ideas you have for each type/method of business.

If, for example, you scored highest in the Information Technology interest area and in the Repair or Build It type, how could you build something new in the field of technology? What are the needs? What has not been done? Then do the same for the other top interest and type combinations.

Highest Interest Area: _____

Entrepreneurial Type	*Business Ideas*
_____	1. _____
	2. _____
	3. _____
_____	1. _____
	2. _____
	3. _____
_____	1. _____
	2. _____
	3. _____

What ideas from this grouping seem most viable for you?

_____

_____

_____

(continued)

Incubating Your Interests (continued)

Now do the same for your second highest interest score from the assessment in this chapter:

Second Highest Interest Area: _____

Entrepreneurial Type	*Business Ideas*
_____	1. _____
	2. _____
	3. _____
_____	1. _____
	2. _____
	3. _____
_____	1. _____
	2. _____
	3. _____

What ideas from this grouping seem most viable for you?

_____

_____

_____

Now do the same for your third highest interest score from the assessment in this chapter:

Third Highest Interest Area: _____

Entrepreneurial Type	*Business Ideas*
_____	1. _____
	2. _____
	3. _____
_____	1. _____
	2. _____
	3. _____

Entrepreneurial Type	**Business Ideas**
_____	1. _____
	2. _____
	3. _____

What ideas from this grouping seem most viable for you?

_____

_____

_____

_____

Now that you have had a chance to explore your interests related to the type of entrepreneur you are, you should have a good understanding of the types of business ideas that appeal to you the most. You should use this list simply as a place to start at this point. Keep in mind any business ideas that at this moment sound like they would be an interesting, viable business for you to begin. However, do not make any immediate decisions about the type of business you would like to begin. In the next chapter, you will go through the same process, this time with your skills.

CHAPTER 5

Assess Your Talents

Now that you have identified your interests, it is time to do the same with your skills. Skills are those things you are good at doing at work, at leisure, and at home. Your skills may correspond with your interests, or they may differ. For example, you may love to work on car engines (high interest), but you might not be very good at it (low skill). If asked about your skills, you would probably be able to name a few. Taking the Entrepreneurial Skills Inventory in this chapter encourages you to think about all of the skills you have used throughout your life.

When you are identifying your skills, remember not to simply think about the paid work you have done. You may also use a variety of skills in your spare time or in time spent with friends and family. For example, if you are the president of the local school PTA, you use a great many different types of skills. Similarly, if you make travel plans for your family, you use a lot of research, coordination, and negotiating skills. At the end of the chapter, these skills become an important factor in helping you to generate more business ideas.

The Entrepreneurial Skills Inventory

The Entrepreneurial Skills Inventory is designed to help you think about and identify the skills you possess that can be transferred to an entrepreneurial venture. These skills may have been acquired from working at various full- or part-time jobs, leisure activities, volunteer experiences, hobbies, educational courses, and training experiences. You might worry about your skills not being good enough to transfer to a business of your own. At this point, do not be too harsh on yourself. Simply reflect back on the skills you have used in the various roles you have played in your life.

Please read each statement carefully. Then, using the following scale, circle the number that best describes your degree of skill:

3 = Very Skilled

2 = Somewhat Skilled

1 = Poorly Skilled

0 = Not Skilled or Not Applicable (N/A)

This is not a test. There are no right or wrong answers, so do not spend too much time thinking about your answers. Be sure to respond to every statement. Do not worry about totaling your scores at this point.

	Very Skilled	Somewhat Skilled	Poorly Skilled	Not Skilled or N/A
In handling plants and animals, how skilled are you at the following tasks?				
1. Feeding and watering	3	2	1	0
2. Weeding	3	2	1	0
3. Grooming pets	3	2	1	0
4. Breeding pets	3	2	1	0
5. Tree trimming	3	2	1	0
6. Planting	3	2	1	0
7. Gardening	3	2	1	0
8. Training pets	3	2	1	0
9. Landscaping	3	2	1	0
10. Farming	3	2	1	0
Section 1 Total: _____				
In working with your hands, how skilled are you at the following tasks?				
11. Building	3	2	1	0
12. Wiring	3	2	1	0
13. Remodeling	3	2	1	0
14. Repairing	3	2	1	0
15. Plumbing	3	2	1	0
16. Wallpapering	3	2	1	0
17. Measuring	3	2	1	0
18. Designing buildings	3	2	1	0
19. Drafting	3	2	1	0
20. Using tools	3	2	1	0
Section 2 Total: _____				

	Very Skilled	Somewhat Skilled	Poorly Skilled	Not Skilled or N/A
In expressing your ideas creatively, how skilled are you at the following tasks?				
21. Singing	3	2	1	0
22. Dancing	3	2	1	0
23. Taking photographs	3	2	1	0
24. Drawing	3	2	1	0
25. Writing	3	2	1	0
26. Performing	3	2	1	0
27. Editing	3	2	1	0
28. Designing	3	2	1	0
29. Painting	3	2	1	0
30. Sculpting	3	2	1	0
Section 3 Total: _____				
In working with others to complete projects, how skilled are you at the following tasks?				
31. Supervising	3	2	1	0
32. Coordinating events	3	2	1	0
33. Planning	3	2	1	0
34. Organizing	3	2	1	0
35. Directing	3	2	1	0
36. Delegating	3	2	1	0
37. Managing	3	2	1	0
38. Bookkeeping	3	2	1	0
39. Filing	3	2	1	0
40. Discharging employees	3	2	1	0
Section 4 Total: _____				
In helping people to learn, how skilled are you at the following tasks?				
41. Tutoring	3	2	1	0
42. Coaching	3	2	1	0
43. Teaching	3	2	1	0
44. Training	3	2	1	0
45. Planning lessons	3	2	1	0
46. Encouraging	3	2	1	0
47. Counseling	3	2	1	0
48. Mentoring	3	2	1	0

(continued)

(continued)

	Very Skilled	Somewhat Skilled	Poorly Skilled	Not Skilled or N/A
49. Testing knowledge	3	2	1	0
50. Explaining ideas	3	2	1	0
Section 5 Total: _____				

In making decisions involving money, how skilled are you at the following tasks?

	Very Skilled	Somewhat Skilled	Poorly Skilled	Not Skilled or N/A
51. Accounting	3	2	1	0
52. Budgeting	3	2	1	0
53. Calculating	3	2	1	0
54. Analyzing data	3	2	1	0
55. Managing inventory	3	2	1	0
56. Auditing	3	2	1	0
57. Financial planning	3	2	1	0
58. Selling	3	2	1	0
59. Investing	3	2	1	0
60. Solving math problems	3	2	1	0
Section 6 Total: _____				

In helping an organization, how skilled are you at the following tasks?

	Very Skilled	Somewhat Skilled	Poorly Skilled	Not Skilled or N/A
61. Campaigning	3	2	1	0
62. Lobbying	3	2	1	0
63. Inspecting	3	2	1	0
64. Planning	3	2	1	0
65. Reporting	3	2	1	0
66. Proofreading	3	2	1	0
67. Compiling statistics	3	2	1	0
68. Entering data	3	2	1	0
69. Keeping records	3	2	1	0
70. Evaluating	3	2	1	0
Section 7 Total: _____				

In helping people to be healthier, how skilled are you at the following tasks?

	Very Skilled	Somewhat Skilled	Poorly Skilled	Not Skilled or N/A
71. Caring for others	3	2	1	0
72. Nursing	3	2	1	0
73. Treating injuries	3	2	1	0
74. Doing research	3	2	1	0
75. Examining specimens	3	2	1	0
76. Diagnosing	3	2	1	0

	Very Skilled	Somewhat Skilled	Poorly Skilled	Not Skilled or N/A
77. Performing experiments	3	2	1	0
78. Healing	3	2	1	0
79. Fixing teeth	3	2	1	0
80. Dispensing medicines	3	2	1	0

Section 8 Total: _____

In helping to meet other people's needs, how skilled are you at the following tasks?

81. Coaching sports	3	2	1	0
82. Entertaining	3	2	1	0
83. Cooking/baking	3	2	1	0
84. Serving others	3	2	1	0
85. Playing sports	3	2	1	0
86. Cleaning	3	2	1	0
87. Nurturing	3	2	1	0
88. Guiding tours	3	2	1	0
89. Planning events	3	2	1	0
90. Traveling	3	2	1	0

Section 9 Total: _____

In helping other people improve their overall well-being, how skilled are you at the following tasks?

91. Counseling	3	2	1	0
92. Monitoring client progress	3	2	1	0
93. Empathizing	3	2	1	0
94. Solving problems	3	2	1	0
95. Mentoring	3	2	1	0
96. Helping the disabled	3	2	1	0
97. Camp counseling	3	2	1	0
98. Facilitating groups	3	2	1	0
99. Listening	3	2	1	0
100. Studying behavior	3	2	1	0

Section 10 Total: _____

(continued)

(continued)

	Very Skilled	Somewhat Skilled	Poorly Skilled	Not Skilled or N/A
In working with computers, how skilled are you at the following tasks?				
101. Programming computers	3	2	1	0
102. Creating Web pages	3	2	1	0
103. Repairing computers	3	2	1	0
104. Analyzing systems	3	2	1	0
105. Analyzing data	3	2	1	0
106. Technical writing	3	2	1	0
107. Designing software	3	2	1	0
108. Applying software	3	2	1	0
109. Maintaining networks	3	2	1	0
110. Securing networks	3	2	1	0
Section 11 Total: _____				
In protecting others, how skilled are you at the following tasks?				
111. Doing research	3	2	1	0
112. Rehabilitating people	3	2	1	0
113. Enforcing regulations	3	2	1	0
114. Investigating	3	2	1	0
115. Guarding	3	2	1	0
116. Inspecting	3	2	1	0
117. Fighting fires	3	2	1	0
118. Defending	3	2	1	0
119. Handling firearms	3	2	1	0
120. Debating	3	2	1	0
Section 12 Total: _____				
In using machines, how skilled are you at the following tasks?				
121. Repairing	3	2	1	0
122. Assembling	3	2	1	0
123. Installing	3	2	1	0
124. Maintaining	3	2	1	0
125. Setting up	3	2	1	0
126. Drilling	3	2	1	0
127. Welding	3	2	1	0
128. Grinding	3	2	1	0

	Very Skilled	Somewhat Skilled	Poorly Skilled	Not Skilled or N/A
129. Forging	3	2	1	0
130. Operating	3	2	1	0
Section 13 Total: _____				

In persuading others, how skilled are you at the following tasks?

131. Marketing	3	2	1	0
132. Influencing	3	2	1	0
133. Promoting products	3	2	1	0
134. Selling	3	2	1	0
135. Demonstrating	3	2	1	0
136. Raising money	3	2	1	0
137. Writing proposals	3	2	1	0
138. Publicizing	3	2	1	0
139. Speaking publicly	3	2	1	0
140. Communicating	3	2	1	0
Section 14 Total: _____				

In working with the sciences, how skilled are you at the following tasks?

141. Teaching	3	2	1	0
142. Inventing	3	2	1	0
143. Discovering	3	2	1	0
144. Hypothesizing	3	2	1	0
145. Conceptualizing	3	2	1	0
146. Formulating	3	2	1	0
147. Reviewing data	3	2	1	0
148. Conducting experiments	3	2	1	0
149. Researching	3	2	1	0
150. Systematizing data	3	2	1	0
Section 15 Total: _____				

In moving people or materials, how skilled are you at the following tasks?

151. Estimating distances	3	2	1	0
152. Pushing clutches	3	2	1	0
153. Driving	3	2	1	0
154. Operating machinery	3	2	1	0

(continued)

(continued)

	Very Skilled	Somewhat Skilled	Poorly Skilled	Not Skilled or N/A
155. Piloting boats	3	2	1	0
156. Navigating ships	3	2	1	0
157. Shipping	3	2	1	0
158. Unloading	3	2	1	0
159. Flying	3	2	1	0
160. Delivering	3	2	1	0
Section 16 Total: _____				

Scoring

The Entrepreneurial Skills Inventory is made up of 16 sections representing the same 16 major career clusters as the Entrepreneurial Interest Inventory in Chapter 4. For each of the 16 sections on the previous pages, add the numbers you circled for each item. Put that total on the line at the end of each section. The higher the total number for each section, the more skilled you are in that particular career cluster:

- A score from 0 to 10 is low.
- A score from 11 to 20 is average.
- A score from 21 to 30 is high.

Matching Your Skills to Businesses

For each of the 16 areas that follow, list your score on the Entrepreneurial Skills Inventory and whether it was low, average, or high:

1. **Agriculture and Natural Resources:** Working with plants, animals, forests, or mineral resources for agriculture, horticulture, conservation, and other purposes.
   Skill: _____

2. **Architecture and Construction:** Designing, assembling, and maintaining buildings and other structures.
   Skill: _____

3. **Arts and Communication:** Creatively expressing feelings or ideas, communicating news or information, or performing.
   Skill: _____

4. **Business and Administration:** Making an organization run smoothly.
   Skill: _____

5. **Education and Training:** Helping people learn.

   Skill: _____

6. **Finance and Insurance:** Helping businesses and people secure their financial future.

   Skill: _____

7. **Government and Public Administration:** Helping a government agency serve the needs of the public.

   Skill: _____

8. **Health Science:** Keeping people and animals healthy.

   Skill: _____

9. **Hospitality, Tourism, and Recreation:** Catering to the wishes and needs of others so that they may enjoy a clean environment, good food and drink, comfortable accommodations, and recreation.

   Skill: _____

10. **Human Service:** Improving people's social, mental, emotional, or spiritual well-being.

    Skill: _____

11. **Information Technology:** Designing, developing, managing, and supporting information systems.

    Skill: _____

12. **Law and Public Safety:** Upholding people's rights or protecting people and property.

    Skill: _____

13. **Manufacturing:** Processing materials into products or maintaining and repairing products by using machines or hand tools.

    Skill: _____

14. **Retail and Wholesale Sales and Service:** Bringing others to a particular point of view through personal persuasion and sales techniques.

    Skill: _____

15. **Scientific Research, Engineering, and Mathematics:** Discovering, collecting, and analyzing information about the natural world, life sciences, and human behavior.

    Skill: _____

16. **Transportation, Distribution, and Logistics:** Moving people or materials.

    Skill: _____

Identifying the Career Clusters That Best Fit Your Skills

Looking back over your results, which of the 16 career clusters yielded the highest total scores? Use the following space to list the three career clusters you scored highest in. This list provides an excellent clue as to the kind of business you will find the most success at owning and operating.

1. _____

2. _____

3. _____

Generating Business Ideas Based on Your Skills

Take a look at the list you made (at the end of Chapter 4) of the three career clusters you are most interested in. How does this list relate to the list you just made of the three career clusters that best fit your skills? Keep in mind that you may have a high interest level in a certain career cluster, but a low skill level. (The opposite also can be true.) You should begin your exploration of potential business options with career clusters in which you have both a high interest level and a high skill level.

The following worksheet will help you to organize your thoughts about business ideas that you are considering. If you need a push to help you generate business ideas, use the same list of questions given in Chapter 4 regarding your interests (these are repeated below). This time, answer these questions based on your primary skills and entrepreneurial type:

- What product or service would make life easier?
- What product or service would make things more convenient?
- What product or service would provide people with a better life?
- What product or service are people complaining about?
- What service could be done more easily?
- What product or service could be provided at a lower cost?
- What products or services are the current trends?
- What product or service could you use in your community?
- What product or service is needed in this economy?

If these questions do not help you to generate ideas for your business, look at the appendix for business ideas related to the career clusters that match your skills.

Focus on Your Skills

At the top of each of the tables that follow, list your highest skill areas (Health Science, Information Technology, and so on) from the Entrepreneurial Skills Inventory you completed in this chapter. In the left-hand column of each table, write your top entrepreneurial types from Chapter 3. Then, in the right-hand column, list all of the potential entrepreneurial ideas you have for each type/method of business. If, for example, you scored highest in the Information Technology interest area and in the Repair or Build It type, how could you build something new in the field of technology? What are the needs? What has not been done? Then do the same for the other top skill and type combinations.

Highest Skill Area: _____

Entrepreneurial Type	**Business Ideas**
_____	1. _____
	2. _____
	3. _____
_____	1. _____
	2. _____
	3. _____
_____	1. _____
	2. _____
	3. _____

What ideas from this grouping seem most viable for you?

_____

_____

_____

(continued)

Focus on Your Skills (continued)

Now do the same for your second highest skill score from the assessment in this chapter:

Second Highest Skill Area: _____

Entrepreneurial Type   *Business Ideas*

_____   1. _____
                           2. _____
                           3. _____

_____   1. _____
                           2. _____
                           3. _____

_____   1. _____
                           2. _____
                           3. _____

What ideas from this grouping seem most viable for you?

_____

_____

_____

Now do the same for your third highest skill score from the assessment in this chapter:

Third Highest Skill Area: _____

Entrepreneurial Type	*Business Ideas*
_____	1. _____
	2. _____
	3. _____
_____	1. _____
	2. _____
	3. _____
_____	1. _____
	2. _____
	3. _____

What ideas from this grouping seem most viable for you?

_____

_____

_____

You now have had an opportunity to explore your interests and skills as they relate to business ideas. This is a big step in your development as an entrepreneur. Without going through this exercise, you might find yourself off track and into a business venture that you neither enjoy nor feel skilled at. Remember that identifying the best business option for you is a combination of right-brain and left-brain thinking. In the last three chapters, you have completed the left-brain, rational exploration of entrepreneurial characteristics. The next chapter is designed to help you combine this information with more right-brain exploration techniques.

CHAPTER 6

Commit to Your Business

Many entrepreneurs become so focused on generating an idea for their business that they fail to commit to making it a reality. The entrepreneurs who are most successful are those who are passionate about their business idea, have confidence in their ability to implement the idea, and are committed to making their business idea a success.

You have probably heard the statistic that 90 percent of all new businesses fail within the first year of operation. You likely have seen evidence of it in your own community when businesses open quickly and then just as quickly close. Often the reason for a new business closing in its first year is a lack of commitment on the part of the entrepreneur. This lack of commitment can be seen in a lack of vision about a product or service, unwillingness to take the necessary risks, and a lack of perseverance when the going gets tough. No matter how great your ideas and innovations are, you cannot succeed if you are not 100 percent committed to your business product or service. It is important that you determine the specific type of product or service that you will feel committed to and passionate about for the long entrepreneurial haul.

Many aspiring entrepreneurs focus on business ideas they think will earn them the most money or are preoccupied with businesses that are successful elsewhere. What you should concentrate on are the skills you already have acquired from work, leisure, or schooling. Remember, the business you begin must be one in which you are skilled and one in which you have interest. When you are interested in your work, you will be

- Committed during the ups and downs of entrepreneurship
- More enthusiastic about your product or service

- Willing to spend more time developing your business
- More knowledgeable about your product/service
- More pleasant to your customers
- More satisfied in your work
- In a position to make more money

These are just some of the reasons that being committed to your business is important. There will certainly be times when you will feel like your business is not going to be profitable or that you may have made a mistake. Every entrepreneur has those feelings at some point. However, when you are committed to your service or your product, you will persevere through the hard times as well as the good times.

The Entrepreneurial Commitment Scale

As an entrepreneur, you will be called upon to do more than come up with great ideas. Business ideas can keep you motivated, but you still need to develop commitment. You don't have to have an MBA from Harvard to be a successful entrepreneur, but you do need to possess certain basic commitment and perseverance traits. The Entrepreneurial Commitment Inventory will help you to determine whether you have what it takes to start your own business and remain committed to it during the roller-coaster ride that is entrepreneurship.

This scale contains 48 statements that are divided into six categories. Read each of the statements and decide how much it describes you. You have four options:

Very Much Like Me

Somewhat Like Me

A Little Like Me

Not Like Me

Circle the number to the right of each statement in the column of the response that best describes you. Note the numbers in the columns vary depending on the statement.

This is not a test. There are no right or wrong answers, so do not spend too much time thinking about your answers. Be sure to respond to every statement.

	Very Much Like Me	Somewhat Like Me	A Little Like Me	Not Like Me
1. I am full of new ideas and dreams.	4	3	2	1
2. I can visualize the future in detail.	4	3	2	1
3. I have no idea about what kind of business I could start.	1	2	3	4
4. I am a dreamer who works to make my dreams come true.	4	3	2	1
5. If I have to change plans, I can come up with alternatives quickly.	4	3	2	1
6. I always look for new ways of doing things.	4	3	2	1
7. I tend to focus on today rather than on long-term dreams.	1	2	3	4
8. I see business opportunities everywhere.	4	3	2	1
Section 1 Total: _____				
9. The cost of starting a business makes me nervous.	1	2	3	4
10. Bearing the consequences of the risks I take does not bother me.	4	3	2	1
11. I believe it is better to have tried and failed than never to have tried.	4	3	2	1
12. I worry about taking a big financial risk in starting a business.	1	2	3	4
13. I worry about the legal issues that accompany a new business.	1	2	3	4
14. I wonder if the effort to start a business is worth the bother or risk.	1	2	3	4
15. I am willing to take risks to earn rewards.	4	3	2	1
16. Fear of failure prevents me from taking business risks.	4	3	2	1
Section 2 Total: _____				
17. I keep working until the task is complete.	4	3	2	1
18. When I set my mind on doing something, I will let nothing stop me.	4	3	2	1
19. When I do something, I always follow through to the end.	4	3	2	1
20. I am able to learn from my failures.	4	3	2	1
21. I abandon projects when I am not successful.	1	2	3	4

(continued)

(continued)

	Very Much Like Me	Somewhat Like Me	A Little Like Me	Not Like Me
22. After setbacks, I try again.	4	3	2	1
23. I can be extremely single-minded and shut out other needs.	4	3	2	1
24. I get irritated when I have to change my plans.	1	2	3	4
Section 3 Total: _____				
25. I have a plan of action before I start a project.	4	3	2	1
26. I am enthusiastic about my ideas and opinions.	4	3	2	1
27. I do not give up at the first sign of trouble.	4	3	2	1
28. I will not allow work to interfere with my hobbies or family.	1	2	3	4
29. I think long and hard about an idea before getting started.	1	2	3	4
30. I am not very competitive in business.	1	2	3	4
31. I think it takes luck to make a new business successful.	1	3	2	4
32. I am committed to being an entrepreneur.	4	3	2	1
Section 4 Total: _____				
33. I do not like to compete with others.	1	2	3	4
34. I like taking action rather than thinking.	4	3	2	1
35. I am more resourceful than most people.	4	3	2	1
36. I am more ambitious than most people.	4	2	3	1
37. I am methodical and strategic.	4	2	3	1
38. I am considered a doer.	4	2	3	1
39. I make decisions quickly and confidently.	4	3	2	1
40. I can focus all my efforts to achieving my goal.	4	3	2	1
Section 5 Total: _____				
41. I'm not sure I have the entrepreneurship traits needed to be successful.	1	2	3	4
42. I am willing to take risks to achieve better things.	4	3	2	1
43. I admit my mistakes and learn from them.	4	3	2	1
44. I am positive I could build a business.	4	3	2	1
45. I handle changing situations with comfort and ease.	4	3	2	1
46. If something looks difficult, I avoid doing it.	1	2	3	4

	Very Much Like Me	Somewhat Like Me	A Little Like Me	Not Like Me
47. I believe that if I work hard, I will succeed.	4	3	2	1
48. When I face difficulty, I feel negative and hopeless.	1	2	3	4
Section 6 Total: _____				

Scoring

The assessment you just completed can help you determine which traits and characteristics you possess that can help you be a successful entrepreneur. For each of the six sections, count the scores you circled. Put that total on the line marked "Total" at the end of each section.

For each section, you will get a score that ranges from 8 to 32.

> Vision (Section 1): _____
>
> Risk Tolerance (Section 2): _____
>
> Perseverance (Section 3): _____
>
> Commitment (Section 4): _____
>
> Goal Orientation (Section 5): _____
>
> Confidence (Section 6): _____

A score from 24 to 32 on a scale is high, indicating that you demonstrate a lot of this trait that is common to successful entrepreneurs. A score from 16 to 23 on a scale indicates that you have a moderate amount of this trait that is common to successful entrepreneurs. Scores from 8 to 15 on a scale are low and indicate that you lack this trait that is common to successful entrepreneurs.

Understanding the Scales

People often ask (and if you are reading this book you are probably asking yourself) "Do I have what it takes to be an entrepreneur?" This is not an easy question to answer. Because entrepreneurs are people who have decided to take control of their future and become self-employed, they tend to possess certain traits, attitudes, and characteristics. You do not need to have a full complement of these traits, attitudes, and characteristics, but it will help you be more successful in the start-up and development of your business. Following are descriptions of the six scales on The Entrepreneurial Commitment Scale.

- **Vision:** High scores on this scale suggest that you have a vision for the future. You are guided by this vision, and your own business is critical in this vision. You are able to see your business's short-term, middle-term, and long-term goals and work to achieve them.

- **Risk Tolerance:** High scores on this scale suggest that you are ready and willing to take calculated risks and face the consequences of those risks. You have the courage to handle failure and start again if you encounter setbacks. You will never give up and are willing to deal with the financial risks involved in starting your own business.

- **Perseverance:** High scores on this scale suggest that you have the determination and persistence to pursue your entrepreneurial goals despite setbacks, barriers, and obstacles you might encounter in your own business. Because you want to succeed in your chosen entrepreneurial venture, you will persist regardless of the obstacles you encounter.

- **Commitment:** High scores on this scale suggest that you are committed to being a successful entrepreneur. You will not give up when your business experiences difficulties. Because you feel destined to achieve your entrepreneurial goals, you will commit to your business.

- **Goal Orientation:** High scores on this scale suggest that you are focused on achieving your entrepreneurial goals. You make decisions quickly and effectively and are constantly thinking about what you can do to achieve your entrepreneurial goals.

- **Confidence:** High scores on this scale suggest that you are confident in your ability to be a successful entrepreneur. Entrepreneurs must exhibit extreme levels of self-confidence in order to manage the risks associated with starting and owning a business, and you exhibit this trait.

If you did not score as high as you hoped on any of the scales of this assessment, do not despair. The traits and attitudes that comprise commitment can be enhanced through awareness and reflection. The activities in the rest of the chapter are designed to help you develop and maintain motivation and a commitment to your dreams and your business.

Building Motivation Through Business Ideas

Motivation is a positive incentive that you can use to help maintain your commitment. For entrepreneurs, motivation often begins in the form of a business idea. When you have a great idea that is new and innovative, you can't wait to get started with your business. The problem is that this motivation often wanes over time.

A great example of the connection between motivation and commitment is the New Year's Eve resolution. If you are like me, every New Year's Eve you make a resolution to do something constructive like lose weight. This great idea motivates you to change your eating for several weeks (or days in my case). Then, when the process starts to get tough and you are tempted by high-calorie foods, you find that you have lost your motivation and decide not to diet anymore. The same thing happens to many entrepreneurs. They develop a great business idea and are excited during the planning and start-up phase. However, when they face obstacles and challenges, they lose their motivation and quit the business. Successful entrepreneurs are able to harness the power of both motivation and commitment.

This section will help you to develop motivation through a careful exploration (using both right-brain and left-brain techniques) of various business ideas you might be considering. Remember, though, that an idea by itself will only take you so far; the rest of the chapter will help you develop commitment to your business idea.

Finding Ideas All Around You

Ideas for businesses are all around you. Everywhere you look and everything you look at should suggest entrepreneurial possibilities. Almost every situation in your community will suggest possible businesses you can own and operate.

For example, if you often "watch" your grandchildren or neighbors' children, would people be willing to pay you for such a service? If you collected baseball cards as a child, how much money would it take for you to start buying and selling cards from your home using your collection as a base from which to get started?

In another example, an unemployed welder (Joe) in my neighborhood was blacktopping his driveway. All of his other neighbors liked the way his driveway looked and wanted theirs to look as good. They asked if he could provide this service to them for a fee. Soon word got around the neighborhood and several other neighborhoods that he provided this service, and Joe was able to earn extra money. Today Joe has his own business providing blacktopping and concrete restoration services in surrounding neighborhoods.

Business Idea Starting Points

Generating business ideas is a must for any business venture. In order to generate ideas for your business, you need to be observant, creative, and knowledgeable. You can find business ideas in all sorts of places. Following are some of the ways you can generate your own business ideas:

- The yellow pages can be an excellent source of ideas for your business. Use it to identify existing businesses in your area that are similar to one you might like to start. How can your business be different from an existing one?

- Magazines and books related to your interests can be chock full of business ideas. Pick up any magazine and look through it. What ideas jump out at you?

- The Internet is full of great ideas. You can simply do a Google search for franchises, for example, and you will get a plethora of new ideas. Search for websites related to your interests. What interesting ideas do you find?

- Read and study as much as you possibly can about your product or service. Go to the local library or bookstore and simply browse. What topics catch your eye?

- Observe what is going on around you. Go to the mall or some other public place. Watch people and notice the trends that you see. What products are people using? How do they dress? Is there a product or service that is essential?

(continued)

Business Idea Starting Points (continued)

- Think creatively about existing products you or your friends use. Are there ways to combine two existing products into one of your own? What is available but is too expensive to be practical? Can you do it for less money? What are the technology (service, educational, and so on) needs of the future?

- Think creatively about the needs of various groups of people. What do babies need? What are the needs of teenagers? Is there a product that parents could use? How can you improve life for the elderly?

Constantly think about new ideas and new ways of doing things. Think about what is needed in your town or community. You should also think about things that could be improved or a service that could be provided in a better way. I suggest that you keep a running list of business ideas in a small notebook that you carry with you.

Brainstorming Business Ideas

Brainstorming is probably the most well-known and widely used technique for generating ideas for new businesses. Brainstorming involves generating all possible entrepreneurial ideas through spontaneous contribution.

In Chapters 3, 4, and 5, you completed the logical (left-brain) exploration of your interests, personality, and skills as they relate to various business ideas. In the following worksheets, I am going to ask you to be creative (right-brain) and allow your subconscious to help you decide on a product or service to market. To do so, you will be relying on insight. Creative insights often arise through thinking about ideas in novel ways.

> **NOTE**
>
> You can generate many more business possibilities if you have family members and friends help you brainstorm.

Identifying Entrepreneurial Possibilities

Write down all business ideas, no matter how illogical they seem, without allowing the critical part of your mind to criticize or evaluate the ideas. Don't limit your thinking. For example, if you are good at gardening, you will probably say to yourself that there are no business opportunities for gardening. However, when you really begin to think about all of the options, there are quite a few. Related businesses include lawn care and tree trimming services, greenhouses, flower shops, landscaping services, and Christmas tree farms.

Use this space to list potential ideas for your business:

_____

_____

_____

Answer the following questions to identify some other possibilities:

1. What did you, as a child, dream of doing when you grew up?

   _____

2. What activity has brought you the most joy over the past 5 years?

   _____

3. Who were your heroes? What about them inspired you?

   _____

4. What type of business would give you the emotional rewards you want?

   _____

5. What leisure activity feels good to you, and is there a similar business to it?

   _____

6. What activity leaves you exhausted when you complete it?

   _____

7. What activity really makes you happy?

   _____

(continued)

Identifying Entrepreneurial Possibilities (continued)

As you try to decide which business idea is best for you to pursue, keep in mind your answers to these questions. Your answers will give you valuable insight into the best type of business for you.

Ranking Business Ideas

For this exercise, list as many possible business ideas as you can, based on the worksheets you completed in Chapters 3, 4, and 5. Then go back over your list and rank the ideas based on the one that seems most viable for you to implement (#1) to the least viable for you to implement.

Rank   **Business Idea**

___   _____

___   _____

___   _____

___   _____

___   _____

___   _____

___   _____

___   _____

___   _____

___   _____

___   _____

___   _____

Describing Your Product or Service

Now it's time to begin to get more specific about the type of product or service you intend to offer. Complete each sentence by filling in the blanks that are provided for you. Review your answers for positive ideas about your product or service.

The product I can make or the service I could provide that others would pay me for is

_____.

I am interested in this opportunity because

_____.

My product or service solves the problem of

_____.

My product or service fills this specific need:

_____.

This product or service is unique because

_____.

My product or service is best described as

_____.

Specific benefits people would derive from my product or service are

1. _____.

2. _____.

3. _____.

The customers who would use my product or service are

_____.

For my product/service, people would pay $ _____.

Now is the perfect time to begin a business because

_____.

The perfect name for my business would be _____.

To begin promoting my product or service, I need to _____

because _____.

Evaluating Your Ideas

Now that you have identified your entrepreneurial type, interests, and skills and brainstormed several business ideas, it is time to get serious about your product or service. To do so, you need to get feedback from others and take a look at the positive and negative aspects of your options. Once you have an idea for the type of business you would like to start, work through the following exercises to help determine whether the idea is feasible.

Getting Feedback

Talk with several trusted relatives or friends. Get their feedback from the standpoint of a customer of the product or service. Encourage them to be as honest as possible. Complete the following table with their feedback.

Person	*Positive Feedback*	*Negative Feedback*

Listing Pros and Cons

Look at some of the advantages and disadvantages of your business idea to determine whether there are more pluses or minuses associated with your idea. Complete the chart that follows. In the left-hand column, list the pros of your idea. In the right-hand column, list the cons.

Pros	*Cons*

Developing Entrepreneurial Commitment

Now that you are motivated by the identification of a business idea, it is time to develop your commitment to your idea(s). Entrepreneurial commitment is the pledge or promise you make to yourself to start and maintain an entrepreneurial venture. Having a great business idea will provide you with the motivation to succeed, but the following activities are designed to help you build up your level of commitment when your motivation begins to wane.

Vision

When you are thinking about ideas for your business, you need to overcome your fear of the unknown and explore new territories. Entrepreneurs often begin with a business idea that is not yet reality but is within their future vision. By overcoming your fear of the unknown, you can develop ideas that are revolutionary.

I was working with a person who wanted to do something with interior design skills, such as offering a service to college students who need help in decorating their dorm rooms and apartments. She kept saying such things as "Nobody would ever want that type of service" and "it has never been done before." Even though she had a vision of what she wanted to do in her business, she kept trying to talk herself out of exploring this new territory. Don't do this to yourself. Embrace your vision and commit to making it happen.

Strengthening Your Vision

Take time to think about the future. The more time you spend considering your ideas about your future, the more vivid your vision will become. Fill in the blanks of this worksheet to start strengthening your vision.

Talk with someone you know who has good implementation skills. Talk with that person about how you could implement your vision. What did that person suggest?

_____

_____

Finish the following statement: My ideal future business would be _____

_____.

Your vision is often tied to your mission statement. What is the mission statement for your future business?

_____

_____

Risk Tolerance

As an entrepreneur, you have to be able to take calculated risks for personal and professional growth. *Calculated risks* are activities that do not have a certain outcome (which for entrepreneurs is about everything!). Having a fear of failure can keep you from taking risks that will help to build your business. The interior designer I talked about in the previous section was afraid of failing because her idea was revolutionary but without a conceivable outcome.

These tips can help you overcome your fear of failure and boost your risk tolerance:

- Realize that risk-taking is a positive experience in and of itself, regardless of the outcome.
- Start by taking smaller risks. With success in smaller risks, you will feel more comfortable taking larger risks.
- Start your business with a partner who assumes some of the risk. Remember, though, that the partner will assume some of the rewards also.
- Consider purchasing a franchise that offers you support and financing while you work at your business.

Perseverance

People with perseverance do not give up when they face obstacles or challenges. They know that their hard work and determination will help them become successful entrepreneurs. They are self-motivated and will continue on in the face of hard times. People with perseverance believe they will succeed.

Identify the reasons why you are motivated to persevere in your future business. The reasons might include the need to be in control of your life and career, the need for autonomy, and the need for additional money. When you are considering business ideas, think about which business will keep you motivated when times are tough. Make a promise to yourself that you will work at your business for at least six months before giving up.

Commitment

Commitment is a pledge or promise you make to yourself in order to maintain your business even when times are lean. Commitment is related to setting and achieving goals for the future and developing a plan for the future.

Affirming Your Commitment

Write about how important the goal of starting your own business is. How will you develop a business but not be distracted by outside events?

_____

_____

_____

What changes will you need to make in your personal life to maintain a commitment to your business?

_____

_____

_____

What changes will you need to make in your work life to maintain a commitment to your business?

_____

_____

_____

Goal Orientation

People who strive for a business that is personally significant tend to be successful. Committed goal pursuit can help entrepreneurs in many different ways, including enhancing self-esteem, stimulating self-confidence, and providing meaning when the business is struggling. Chapter 11 has more detailed information on how to set goals. For now, start developing your goals by completing the following worksheet.

Establishing a Goal

Right now, what is your overall business goal?

_____

_____

_____

Break down your overall business goal into "baby steps":

1. _____

2. _____

3. _____

4. _____

Describe your goals in concrete terms:

_____

_____

Confidence

We are not born with self-confidence; we learn and develop self-confidence from our interactions with other people. In other words, self-confidence can be learned and unlearned. As an entrepreneur, you will need to maintain confidence in yourself and your ability to deliver a quality product or service.

Boosting Your Confidence

Think about the people you know who appear to have self-confidence. List three people who, by your observations and by their mannerisms, could be role models of self-confidence. These people may be dead or alive, famous people from history, or people in your life now.

1. _____

2. _____

3. _____

One way you can develop greater self-confidence is by not comparing yourself negatively with other people. Who are the people with whom you typically compare yourself?

_____

_____

_____

_____

Why do you do this?

_____

_____

_____

_____

Remember your successes from the past. Success breeds increased sense-of-self and wself-esteem. What have been your greatest successes?

_____

_____

_____

_____

Having good ideas alone is not enough. Many entrepreneurs stop there and then wonder why their businesses do not take form. These ideas must be formed into a viable business enterprise. Do not worry about which business ideas are the most profitable at this time, but rather focus on the ideas which excite your imagination. Think about the types of businesses for which you would have the most passion and commitment. If you are doing the things you enjoy, you will make lots of money doing them. The next part will help you to identify a structure for implementing your business ideas and help you begin to develop your own business plan.

PART 3: PLANNING YOUR BUSINESS

"The critical ingredient is getting off your butt and doing something. It's as simple as that. A lot of people have ideas, but there are few who decide to do something about them now. Not tomorrow. Not next week. But today. The true entrepreneur is a doer, not a dreamer."

—*Nolan Bushnell*

CHAPTER 7

Implement Your Choice

A lot of people have a true desire to become an entrepreneur. They have a great idea, some money set aside, and a big dream. But entrepreneurship is much more than having a great idea—you have to have a plan for getting the idea to the marketplace. This statement is true whether you are planning to purchase a franchise or start your own home-based business.

You probably have many of the aspects of your business plan already developed, at least in your mind. You have generated business ideas, thought about the product or service you want to offer, and thought about who your potential customers will be. But you may not have thought about such things as insurance, marketing, and legal matters. Writing a business plan will force you to put together all of the important aspects of your business.

Business plans follow a specific format that is recognized throughout the business world. A business plan makes you consider your idea from a long-term perspective. It takes a lot of work because you must think about your product or service in terms of your market, operations, and the management of your business.

Business plans help make your idea a reality by

- Providing a framework for your business. Business plans help you to explore the details of your business idea and move the idea to its implementation.

- Driving you to make plans and prepare to set goals. Business plans stop you from charging ahead before you are ready.

- Forcing you to think about aspects of your business that may not be fun for you but need doing. Business plans provide you with a living document that can be revised and updated based on changes in the environment.

- Allowing you to reflect on all aspects of your business before beginning the implementation process.

- Helping you to explore your financial situation and project costs that you may not have considered. Business plans can provide you with information to discover whether your business has a good chance of succeeding.

- Revealing opportunities and innovations that you may not have thought of.

- Providing others (investors, bankers, suppliers, potential partners) with the necessary information about your business.

Guaranteed Success?

Preparing and adhering to a business plan greatly enhances the chances that your new venture will be successful. A business plan will not guarantee that your business is a success, but it will reduce your risk of failure by forcing you to think logically and carefully about your business model and format. However, some successful businesses have started without a business plan. Such businesses include Crate and Barrel, Pizza Hut, and Reebok.

This part of the book (Chapters 7, 8, and 9) is devoted to helping you develop your business plan. Because writing a business plan is a complicated and long process, it has been divided into three sections. Each chapter in this part of the book includes business planning activities and exercises. Therefore, when you have completed the three chapters in this part, you will have developed your comprehensive business plan.

The first, and often most important, aspect of beginning your business plan is to identify the structure for your business. The quiz in this chapter, the Entrepreneurial Implementation Scale, is designed to help you do just that. As you will see, there are many different structures you can use to get your idea out to the masses. By determining your preferred structure, you will be better poised to succeed in the tough world of self-employment. After you have completed the quiz, you will have an opportunity to start creating your own business plan.

The Entrepreneurial Implementation Scale

The Entrepreneurial Implementation Scale will help you explore the best way for you to implement your business idea. Keep in mind that all of the different types of entrepreneurs described in this quiz can be successful. The secret is to find the structure or implementation type that fits your product or service, financial situation, and personal characteristics.

This quiz contains 36 statements. Read each of the statements and circle the number in the Yes column if the statement describes you. If the statement does not describe you, circle the number in the No column.

This is not a test, and there are no right or wrong answers. Do not spend too much time thinking about your answers. Your initial response will likely be the most true for you. Be sure to respond to every statement.

	Yes	No
1. I want to start from scratch and build something.	2	1
2. I want the business I operate to be my business.	2	1
3. I want to make important decisions about my business.	2	1
4. I want to operate my business out of a storefront.	2	1
5. I have a talent or passion that people are interested in.	2	1
6. I don't want to operate something built by someone else.	2	1
Section 1 Total: _____		
7. I want to work in a system selling products already developed.	2	1
8. I want to buy an established customer base.	2	1
9. I want to take over an operation that is already successful.	2	1
10. I don't want to start from scratch.	2	1
11. I want to operate an established business.	2	1
12. I want a proven system.	2	1
Section 2 Total: _____		
13. I want to be paid to offer advice.	2	1
14. Others often come to me for business guidance.	2	1
15. I have an expertise that people pay for.	2	1
16. I want to help improve the operations of a business.	2	1
17. I have a specialty that people seek out.	2	1
18. I want to work for multiple clients at the same time.	2	1
Section 3 Total: _____		
19. I want to run an outlet of a chain for my business.	2	1
20. I don't mind paying franchise fees if I get lots of business.	2	1
21. I would prefer working from a proven business model.	2	1

(continued)

(continued)

22.	I want to purchase an established brand name.	2	1
23.	I want a "turnkey operation" to begin immediately.	2	1
24.	I want training in a proven system.	2	1
	Section 4 Total: _____		
25.	I like to do my work in cyberspace.	2	1
26.	I prefer to fill orders from a website.	2	1
27.	I have an Internet-based solution for my business.	2	1
28.	I believe that I can sell objects using technology.	2	1
29.	I like to blog and use social media to sell products/services.	2	1
30.	I know I could successfully market my business online.	2	1
	Section 5 Total: _____		
31.	I want to work out of my house.	2	1
32.	I cannot afford an expensive office right now.	2	1
33.	I see my business as a second source of income.	2	1
34.	I have checked local zoning considerations.	2	1
35.	I am very self-motivated and self-disciplined.	2	1
36.	My product or business can be sold without office space.	2	1
	Section 6 Total: _____		

Scoring

When you become an entrepreneur, the first decision that you must make as part of your business plan is how you will implement your business idea. The Entrepreneurial Implementation Scale is designed to help you identify the best way for you to start your business venture.

For each group of items on the assessment, add the numbers that you circled. This will allow you to get your total scores for each section. You will get a total in the range from 6 to 12. Put that number in the space marked "Total" at the end of each section. Do that for all of the sections. Then transfer these totals to the spaces below:

> Starting from Scratch (Section 1) Total: _____
>
> Buying an Existing Business (Section 2) Total: _____
>
> Consulting (Section 3) Total: _____
>
> Franchise (Section 4) Total: _____
>
> E-business (Section 5) Total: _____
>
> Home-Based Business (Section 6) Total: _____

A high score of 11 or 12 in any section indicates that that method for implementing your business idea will probably be a successful one for you. If you score between 8 and 10 on any scale, that method for implementing your business idea will probably be somewhat successful for you, but watch out for red flags listed later in this chapter. If your score is 6 or 7, this suggests that that method for implementing your business idea probably will not be successful for you.

Selecting a Business Method

Most entrepreneurs are proud of their unique lifestyle. They are proud of their work in a way that nobody working for someone else could be. They attempt to make a satisfying life, not a living. There is a big difference. Making a living suggests paying the bills, saving to send the kids to college, and saving some for retirement. Making a life means making money at something you love, not being tied to an eight-hours-a-day job, taking time off when you want to, not having to commute to work, and spending more time with your family.

The lifestyle you desire has a lot to do with how you will decide to implement your business idea. Some entrepreneurs want to work out of their home and work in their pajamas every day, while others prefer to purchase a franchise and buy a building from which to operate it. I have worked in my business from my house for about 20 years now. My friend Jack turned a hobby of growing houseplants into a full-time business operation. He had a small greenhouse in his backyard where he would grow plants and flowers. He put out a sign and started selling his plants and flowers on Saturdays and in the evenings. Eventually he was able to purchase a small building from which he could sell his products.

Remember that the business plan is a detailed map of your entrepreneurial venture, so you need to carefully consider the form your business will take. Think about how you will make your product or service available to your customers. There are many ways to get your idea to market, and each one has its strengths and red flags. None of the methods described in this chapter is better than the others. Any one of them can be effective if it suits your needs and lifestyle interests. The assessment you just completed was designed to help you determine which method is best for you. The following sections provide more information on each of these methods.

Starting from Scratch

"Starting from scratch" entrepreneurs have an idea for a product or service and want to build their own business from the ground up. They want to make the decisions, take responsibility for how their business turns out, and take pride in their ability to start from scratch and develop their business sale by sale. They often want to have a traditional, bricks-and-mortar business that they could run from a building or storefront.

People starting their own business from scratch often face an uphill battle. Research about new business start-ups suggests that four out of every five new businesses fail within the first five years of operation. The success-to-failure ratio has not improved even though the number of new entrepreneurs has soared. If you are thinking about starting your business from scratch, you need to be cognizant of these statistics. For you, completion of the business plan in these three chapters is the best way to ensure that your start-up venture will succeed.

If you want to start a business from scratch, make sure you can answer yes to these questions:

- Do you have a great idea for a product or service business?
- Have you completed a "needs survey" of local market conditions?
- Do you have a location picked out for your business?
- Have you considered how much it will cost to start your business?
- Do you have a mentor who can help you with the start-up?
- Do you have the time and energy to put in the hours that are required in starting a business from scratch?
- Do you have an established network through which you can advertise your business product or service?

Starting a Business from Scratch Red Flags

Watch for these signals that this business option might not work out for you:

- You are having a hard time developing your business plan.
- You are having a hard time finding a good location.
- You don't feel like you have the energy it will take to start a business from scratch.
- You feel like you need the support that other business options offer.
- You wonder if you have the work ethic it will take to begin from scratch.

Buying an Existing Business

If you don't think that you are cut out to start your own business, but still want to be an entrepreneur, you might think about buying an existing business. Such a business already has an established customer base, a marketing plan, and a financial plan in place, which can save you time and money over starting a business from scratch. Unlike the poor success rates for people starting their own business, more than 50 percent of all businesses acquired by a new owner tend to survive for at least five years or more. This makes this option much less risky and more appealing to some entrepreneurs.

If you are thinking about acquiring an existing business, you still need to do a lot of detective work to be successful. By working through the business planning aspects of this book, you will ensure a successful purchase.

Consider the following questions:

- Do you have the necessary skills and interests for a business in this industry? For example, if you are thinking about purchasing a dog obedience business, you need to make sure that you are interested in animals and are skilled enough to operate the business.

- Do you have the necessary business skills in finance, marketing, and sales for this industry?

- Is there a continuing need for this type of business?

- Are there customers in your area who need this product or service?

- Is it a regional, national, or international business?

- Will you need to continue purchasing inventory for this business?

- Why are the owners selling the business?

Buying an Existing Business Red Flags

Watch for these signals that this business option might not work out for you:

- You get a bad feeling in your gut.
- The earnings claims seem to be larger than others you have researched.
- You are pressured to quickly buy into the business before doing your research.
- You are told that the product or service sells itself.
- You are distracted from talking to others involved in the business.
- You are discouraged from letting your attorney review the contract.

Consulting

Many people who start their own business begin as a consultant. Consultants basically are paid to solve a problem, give advice, or offer guidance to other businesses. They are paid to bring their specific expertise to a business situation and make recommendations for improving or realizing a change. A consulting business is much like a start-from-scratch business, with the only difference being the product is your advice.

Consultants typically are hired to provide their expertise in an area that is absent from a particular business environment. Consultants could provide any of the following types of work:

- Develop and implement recommendations for improvement.
- Investigate a business situation and suggest plans for change.
- Formulate a revision for long-lasting change and improvement.
- Make formal presentations of their conclusions and recommendations.
- Advise administrators about how to fix existing problems.

Consultants provide an external, objective perspective on the existing business system and make recommendations for improving the system. Some consultants are hired for relatively short periods of time to work in businesses that are inadequately staffed. One human resource consultant I know has worked for an organization that does not have employees with the necessary skills or knowledge required to complete a specific project.

Consulting Must-Haves

In order for consulting to work for you, you must fit the following criteria:

- You must have significant experience and a proven track record of success in your specialty.
- You must be attentive to details.
- You must be willing to work for numerous bosses in the form of clients.
- You must be a good networker and be proficient in marketing your services or product. Consultants rely on advertising.

Franchise

When you think of the word *franchise*, you typically think of McDonald's or Wendy's. However, there are many diverse types of franchises including printing companies, maid services, carpet businesses, lawn-care businesses, retail specialty stores, and many more. In franchising, a franchiser owns a business or trademark that has been adopted and is well known in America. You, the franchisee, would then purchase the right to use the trademark and the system of business of the franchiser. You are purchasing the complete system of doing business. You would also receive assistance with site selection for your business, training, advertising, and product supply. For these services, you usually pay up-front franchise fees as well as ongoing royalty fees.

The cost of franchises range in price based primarily on the size of the franchise, its yearly revenues, its history of success, the number of franchises available and in operation, and the location of the franchise you want to purchase. You should choose a franchise based on your interests and financial capabilities. Franchises range in price anywhere from around $2,500 to well over a million dollars for some larger franchises. Some franchises require owners to pay back 5 to 10 percent of the business revenues in royalties to the franchisor.

Most people choose to purchase a franchise because they feel they are starting their business with an established system. The other attractive feature of franchising is the fact that the franchiser is available if questions or problems arise. Franchises also offer name recognition for your business. For example, would you rather go to McDonald's or Joe's Hamburger Stand for lunch?

However, franchisees do not experience complete independence because they are not able to do everything their own way. They must abide by the franchise's operating principles. In addition, franchisees put in a tremendous time commitment, with some spending 12–15 hours a day working to keep the business viable and successful.

If you are thinking about buying a franchise, consider the following:

- Can you afford the franchise?
- Do you want to be tied in completely to the franchisor's system?
- Does the franchise have a track record for success?
- Will your family support you in this venture?
- Do you have realistic expectations about how long it takes to start a successful franchise business?
- Are you willing to take risks?
- What types of financing are available?

Also, if you are planning to purchase a franchise, you should seek advice from people who are already franchisees of the business. Most legitimate franchisors will provide you with the names of some of their franchisees to contact. Here are some questions you should ask:

- What is the nature of the work?
- How long did it take to get established?
- How long did it take to begin making a profit?
- Would they purchase this franchise if they had to do it again?
- Are they satisfied with this franchise?
- How well do they work with the franchisor?
- Is there sufficient support from the franchisor?

Franchising Information

You can find information about franchising at the following websites:

- **www.franchise.com:** Available franchises you can explore and purchase
- **www.franchise.org:** International Franchise Association
- **www.worldfranchising.com:** Information about the world of franchising
- **www.franchisedirect.com:** Directory of franchises for sale

---

Franchise Red Flags

Watch for these signals that this business option might not work out for you:

- The franchise has been around for only a few years.
- The franchise has only a limited number of franchisees.
- You don't receive a copy of the disclosure documents required by law.
- You're pressured into signing a franchise agreement without reviewing it with your attorney.

E-business

The Internet has created a new breed of entrepreneur—the virtual entrepreneur. This type of entrepreneur uses electronic commerce, the Internet, and technology in general to create a competitive advantage in the marketplace. Virtual entrepreneurs operate businesses that have no traditional, bricks-and-mortar location for customers to visit. They do not go out and consult or buy a franchise created by someone else. What sets these entrepreneurs apart is that they rely on technology to do their work. They are proficient at using such technology as websites, e-storefronts, blogging, and social media sites to attract customers to their website. They then are able to harness the power and effectiveness of technology to provide their customers with their product or service. They may have employees, warehouse space, and even an office, but no customers see any of these. These entrepreneurs work with suppliers, develop products, and deliver goods to customers all through using the Internet.

Famous E-businesses

There are many e-businesses that are successful in selling a product or service, including the following:

- Amazon.com

- Monster.com

- Quickenmortgage.com

- 1800flowers.com

Many e-businesses have replaced the traditional bricks-and-mortar businesses. One of the reasons for the success of e-businesses is their ability to provide customers with a product or service almost instantaneously. Now the small business that publishes its own business books can make them available to everyone to download at a moment's notice. The Internet has evened the playing field for small businesses competing with larger, well-established businesses.

E-businesses tend to operate in a variety of ways. Here are five of the most popular models:

- **Subscription model.** This type of e-business charges users a fee to use its service. For example, an entrepreneur with this type of business may charge users every time they ask for advice about a specific topic.

- **Advertising model.** This type of e-business operates by selling advertising on its site. This model is particularly effective for e-businesses that generate a lot of website traffic.

- **Merchant model.** This type of e-business operates by selling products and/or services to buyers through a website. For example, an entrepreneur with this type of business might sell motivational tapes developed in house or resell ones for another manufacturer of the product.

- **Brokerage model.** This type of e-business operates by bringing together buyers and sellers for a fee. For example, an entrepreneur with this type of business might bring together people who want to vacation in Europe with European vacation planners.

- **Business-to-business model.** This type of e-business operates by online transactions between the entrepreneurial business and other businesses. For example, an entrepreneur with this type of business might sell a way to manage meetings more effectively and provide the tool electronically to other businesses around the world.

Regardless of the model you plan to use for your e-business, you should remember to start simple, market a product or service you love, and network in person and on social network sites as much as you possibly can.

Also, consider the following questions:

- Do you have a website that will accommodate all your content, inventory, and customers?
- Do you have an e-commerce system through which customers will feel comfortable entering credit card information?
- Will customers be able to access your product or service easily?
- Will shipping costs be a hindrance for you and customers?
- How will you handle returns and exchanges?
- Will you offer special savings or coupons for shopping online?

E-business Red Flags

Watch for these signals that this business option might not work out for you:

- You lack the skills to manage an e-commerce or e-business online site.
- You have difficulty adapting rapidly to changing website and e-commerce technology.
- You are not sure how to protect the online security of your business and your customers.
- Your product or service does not lend itself well to an e-business format.

Home-Based Business

Working at home is not a new trend. For centuries a variety of people have worked out of their homes either on a full- or part-time basis. Within the last century, though, the number of people choosing to earn a living from working at home has significantly increased. Home-based operations have recently become a legitimate place of business.

Starting a home-based business can be an exciting opportunity and is an excellent way to start creating your own job without all of the expense of entrepreneurship. You can start from scratch or buy a business that already exists. The key factor is that these types of businesses eliminate all the expense of commuting, eating lunch out, driving to work, and sitting in traffic. Your only commute would be from your bedroom in the morning to your home-based office.

Many professional services now being operated from homes include counseling, answering services, legal work, cabinetry, medical billing, information brokering, and catering, just to name a few. I am friends with a young man who was working as a fiscal auditor for a county government agency. Although earning a comfortable living, he was not satisfied at work. In his leisure time, he enjoyed studying investments and investing his money in various financial ventures. As his success grew in these financial ventures, word spread, and soon others were coming to him regarding their financial planning. Approximately one year later, he opened his own financial-planning office from his home and is very satisfied with his new work.

The wide variety of home-based business opportunities provides good news for people interested in this business structure. In a home-based business, you are the boss and can individually determine the work you do, how it is done, and the direction it will take. You also receive all of the benefits of your hard work. Most home-based business owners love having the flexibility in where they work from, how they do the work, and how much time they spend working. In addition, home-based business owners love the fact that they get to choose their clients and customers.

Common Home-Based Business Scams

If you are asked to pay a fee for any of these home-based business opportunities, you should beware:

- Stuffing envelopes
- Clipping coupons
- Assembling products
- Restocking vending machines
- Selling through kiosks
- Selling through storefronts

Home-Based Business Red Flags

Watch for these signals that this business option might not work out for you:

- Your home is full of distractions. Children, pets, televisions, and the Internet can pull you away from your work at home.
- Motivation is an issue for you. Being the boss of your own home-based business requires you to motivate yourself.
- Your business idea will require a lot of space or multiple people to implement it. Home-based businesses are usually small businesses.
- You need interaction with coworkers.

Beginning Your Business Plan

In order to start a business, you will need many key components:

- If you are planning to offer a product, you will need a product supplier. This product might be one that you develop yourself and have manufactured, or it might be one that is manufactured by someone else and you merely sell it for a profit. You can also consider using a wholesaler or manufacturer that sends their products (drop-ships) to customers for you.

- If you are planning to offer a service, you will need to develop a way to provide customers with this service.

- You will need office equipment including a computer, e-commerce software, printer, fax machine, copier, shipping materials (for products sold), and maybe even a separate business phone line if you are working from home.

- You will need to create a website for greater exposure for your business. You can either hire a web design firm or create your own simple website for a small fee. You will need to purchase a website address and domain name (for example, www.mybusiness.com) as well as a website hosting business to host your website.

- You will need to create a marketing plan to promote your business. You will have to think about the best methods for advertising your product or service. (This topic is covered in Chapter 8.)

Setting a framework enables you to begin putting your ideas into practice. The worksheet that follows will help you to sort out what you have learned about yourself in this chapter and identify a potential business structure.

Small Business Services

Following are some of the business services you may want to consult as you begin to build your business plan:

- **Small Business Administration (www.sba.gov):** The Small Business Administration (SBA) is a federal agency that provides business planning services and financial assistance to entrepreneurs. The SBA also offers a host of consulting services, training programs, and information at a minimum cost. In addition, the SBA offers a variety of small business funding programs for start-up capital and ongoing expenses.

- **SCORE (www.score.org):** The Service Corp of Retired Executives (SCORE) provides individual counseling to prospective entrepreneurs at no cost. They also provide business-planning workshops that you can attend for a nominal fee.

- **Small Business Development Center:** The Small Business Development Center, a cooperative venture between the SBA and various community businesses, also provides valuable information and counseling in planning and launching a small business. You can reach the Small Business Development Center through the SBA in your state.

Business Plan, Part 1: Your Business Structure

Structure: This section describes the structure (start from scratch; buy an existing business; consult; or buy a franchise, e-business, or home-based business) you have chosen for implementing your business idea.

Which of the structures discussed in this chapter best suits your needs and lifestyle?

_____

_____

_____

Why do you think this structure is best for you?

_____

_____

_____

What type of product(s) and/or service(s) do you plan to offer?

_____

_____

_____

(continued)

Business Plan, Part 1: Your Business Structure (continued)

Positive aspects of the business structure for me:

_____

_____

_____

Negative aspects of the business structure for me:

_____

_____

_____

Steps I will take to begin implementing my business using this structure:

_____

_____

_____

This chapter was created to help you think about the various ways available for you to implement your business idea. Hopefully, you were able to identify a structure that you feel is the best way for you to take your idea to market and provide your product or service to your customers. The next chapter will help you develop the second section of your business plan and create a marketing and sales approach for your business.

CHAPTER 8

Develop a Sales and Marketing Plan

Now that you have identified a business idea and figured out a way to implement it, it's time to spread the word to others about your product or service. After all, you can have the most amazing product or service in the world, but if you are not able to market it and sell it, potential customers will never find it, nobody will purchase it, and you will not be a successful entrepreneur.

Sales and marketing will most likely be the lifeblood of your business. The secret to any new business is the fact that nothing happens, and you make no money, unless you sell something. Cultivating and connecting with customers and clients in an attempt to build a customer base is imperative for the start and growth of your business. Marketing covers a broad range of activities, all geared to entice customers to purchase your product or service. These sales and marketing aspects of your business make up the second component of your overall business plan.

Developing a comprehensive and effective sales and marketing plan can be difficult. There is no single prescribed sales and marketing strategy that will guarantee the success of your business. For example, effective sales and marketing can take place by word of mouth, the Internet, and print advertising. In this chapter, you will assess your current sales and marketing plans and create a sales and marketing strategy for your business.

What's Your Niche?

Competing with other business owners who offer similar products and services to yours can slow your business growth. To overcome the problems that accompany too much competition, consider carving out a unique business niche in one of the following ways:

- **Offer a product or service that nobody else offers.** When you have something that nobody else can duplicate, you will have a solid grasp on the market. How is your service or product unique?

- **Offer a specialized service or product.** Don't spread yourself too thin. Instead, specialize in one product or service that is as unique as possible.

- **Identify and serve an unserved market.** Think about the markets related to your product or service that are yet unserved. Carve out a niche for yourself by serving this population.

The Sales and Marketing Scale

The Sales and Marketing Scale is designed to help you identify the status of the sales and marketing aspects of your business. This information will be important as you develop your overall business plan.

This assessment contains 30 statements divided into 6 areas that represent the health of your sales and marketing. Read each statement and decide the extent to which the statement describes you and your business at this point in time. Then circle the number in the column that best matches that decision:

3 = Very Descriptive

2 = A Little Descriptive

1 = Not At All Descriptive

This is not a test, and there are no right or wrong answers. Do not spend too much time thinking about your answers. Your initial response will be the most true for you. Be sure to respond to every statement.

	Very Descriptive	Somewhat Descriptive	Not At All Descriptive
In my business, . . .			
1. I have a structured marketing system.	3	2	1
2. I have researched my potential market.	3	2	1
3. I know who my primary target market is.	3	2	1
4. I have a unique message that I present to my target market.	3	2	1
5. I use a variety of marketing techniques to convey my message.	3	2	1
Section 1 Total: _____			
In my business, . . .			
6. I offer a free newsletter, products, or e-zine.	3	2	1
7. I enjoy networking and talking with people.	3	2	1
8. I spend at least half of my time actively selling my product or service.	3	2	1
9. I am a natural salesperson.	3	2	1
10. I enjoy selling my products using social media and the Internet.	3	2	1
Section 2 Total: _____			
In my business, . . .			
11. I have great customer service skills.	3	2	1
12. I understand what my customers need and I provide it.	3	2	1
13. I have researched my potential customer base.	3	2	1
14. I have built my marketing strategy around my customers' needs.	3	2	1
15. I am able to put my product or service in front of my customers.	3	2	1
Section 3 Total: _____			
In my business, . . .			
16. I know which companies dominate the industry.	3	2	1
17. I have purchased my competitor's product/service.	3	2	1
18. I have identified how my product/service is different from that of the competition.	3	2	1

(continued)

(continued)

	Very Descriptive	Somewhat Descriptive	Not At All Descriptive
In my business, . . .			
19. I have researched my competitors.	3	2	1
20. I have researched my competition's marketing strategy.	3	2	1
Section 4 Total: _____			
In my business, . . .			
21. I have a unique brand to identify my product or service.	3	2	1
22. I have a unique logo that my customers recognize.	3	2	1
23. I have developed a brand-building campaign.	3	2	1
24. I understand what my brand should represent.	3	2	1
25. I have a catchy tagline that represents my business.	3	2	1
Section 5 Total: _____			
In my business, . . .			
26. I have an effective website.	3	2	1
27. I have an effective website domain name.	3	2	1
28. I have a cost-effective web hosting service.	3	2	1
29. I blog and use discussion boards to promote my business.	3	2	1
30. I have an electronic storefront of products I market.	3	2	1
Section 6 Total: _____			

Scoring

The Sales and Marketing Scale provides you with information about how you are (or will be) doing at the sales and marketing aspects of your business. Add the numbers you have circled for each of the six sections on the previous pages. Put that total on the line marked "Total" at the end of each section. Transfer your totals for each of the six sections to the lines below:

> Marketing (Section 1) Total: _____
>
> Sales (Section 2) Total: _____
>
> Customers (Section 3) Total: _____
>
> Competitors (Section 4) Total: _____

Branding (Section 5) Total: _____

Technology (Section 6) Total: _____

Your score for each scale will fall into one of the following ranges:

- A score of 5 to 8 indicates that this aspect of the sales and marketing of your business is not healthy. You need to work at enhancing the health of your business in this area.

- A score of 9 to 11 indicates that this aspect of your sales and marketing plan is somewhat healthy. However, you need to continue working to enhance this area of your business.

- A score of 12 to 15 indicates that the sales and marketing aspects of your business tend to be healthy. The activities included will help you to be even more successful at sales and marketing.

Marketing and Sales

Marketing and sales are the critical links of your business to customers and prospective customers. In the end, your business revenues will come from people buying your product or service, and the way people find your business is through your marketing and sales efforts. You should, however, not get confused about these two concepts. Marketing deals with targeting people who need your product or service and getting them to seek you out. Sales is the final transaction in which you get the prospective customer to make a purchase. Following are some marketing and sales strategies you can use:

- **Tell everyone you know about your product or service.** Get word-of-mouth marketing to work for you by being active in the community and networking. Do presentations for potential customers—free talks and seminars can be one of the most effective ways of getting information out about your business and generating referrals.

- **Brush up on and use your writing skills.** You can write ads, blog, develop website copy, and create press releases about your business.

- **Sell your products through a retail store.** Contact retail outlets with samples of your product and persuade the store managers to buy it. Or you could also lease space in a store where you can sell the product yourself.

Customers

Getting to know your customers is important. Without them, you will not have a business for long. To develop a loyal customer base, you need to reflect on who your typical customers are or will be.

Understanding the Demographics of Your Target Market

How would you define your target market? Who are all of the possible people who might buy your product or service?

_____

_____

How large is the market (the total estimate of the size of the market) for your product or service?

_____

_____

What research and statistics do you have to confirm your market?

_____

_____

Fill in the blanks for the customers in your target market:

Age: _____   Sex: _____

Family Status: _____

Occupation: _____

Income Level: _____

Geographic Location: _____

Physical Characteristics: _____

Other: _____

Competition

It is important to know your customers, but it also is important to know your competitors. When I first began my career assessment business, there were no (or very few) competitors. With the increased interest in all types of assessment and the advent of the Internet, more people have broken into the assessment industry. This competition has changed the way that I do business. For example,

I have thoroughly researched the new assessment businesses that have opened, and I continue to monitor their activities through their websites and by surfing such company data sites as www.about. com, www.lexis-nexis.com, and www.onesource.com. By researching my competition, I am able to find out information about their customer bases, their marketing strategies, their pricing structures, and their customer service strategies. I am also able to develop ideas for new products by exploring their product offerings.

The nature and scope of your competition will have a major impact on the level of your business sales. The following worksheet is designed to help you systematically look at your top competitors.

Sizing Up the Competition

Who are your major competitors? List them below and fill out the information for each one.

Competitor	Product/Service	Strengths	Weaknesses
_____	_____	_____	_____
_____	_____	_____	_____
_____	_____	_____	_____
_____	_____	_____	_____
_____	_____	_____	_____
_____	_____	_____	_____

Based on the list of competitors you generated, answer the following questions:

1. How is your product or service different from that of your competitors? How will you compete with them?

   _____

2. What difficulties do you envision?

   _____

3. Why will you be successful?

   _____

4. What marketing strategies do your competitors use?

   _____

(continued)

Sizing Up the Competition (continued)

5. How is their pricing structure different from yours?

_____

6. How do your competitors serve their customers?

_____

Branding

Now that you are in the process of developing a marketing strategy, you can start thinking about your brand. Brands are labels used by your business to make your product or service distinctive from the products and services of your competitors. Your brand is what identifies your offerings and could include your logo, advertising materials, website, and the uniqueness of your product or service. What is the brand of your business or prospective business? The next two worksheets will help you to answer that question.

Brainstorming Your Brand

To help you discover your brand, think of keywords that describe your business. This exercise may help to jog your memory and creativity. My list included the following words:

assessments, career development, practical, community oriented, all things assessment, professional, available, fun, quizzes

Write your keywords here:

_____   _____

_____   _____

_____   _____

_____   _____

_____   _____

_____   _____

What images do those words conjure up for you?

_____

_____

_____

_____

What visual concepts could your customers generate from this list of words?

_____

_____

_____

_____

What words or images would encourage your customers to buy from you? (Use your customer research to help you answer this question.)

_____

_____

_____

_____

Think about what others say about you. List some of those sayings:

_____

_____

_____

_____

Branding involves creating the most memorable image that tells your customers what your business is. Your brand should create a buzz that will get your business noticed by customers. It will include a "catchy" name that will become synonymous with the product or service you offer. For example, when you think of Starbucks, a picture of high-end, quality coffee drinks come into your mind.

Branding is more than the name you put on your letterhead and business cards. Your brand is what you have to offer, your uniqueness, and your promise to your customers.

The following worksheet will help you put the information from the previous worksheet into practice.

Naming Your Business

Naming your business can be one of the most critical and enjoyable parts of the organization of your business. You should choose your business name carefully. The name of your business should provide people with some idea of the nature of your business, conjure up a specific image, and be able to grow as your business grows.

List several qualities that describe your business:

1. _____

2. _____

3. _____

4. _____

What image do you want to portray?

_____

_____

_____

What is your competitive advantage (this is what you do better than the competition)?

_____

_____

_____

What do you think your business color scheme should be?

_____

_____

_____

What symbols, related to your business, do you want your customers to remember?

_____

_____

_____

List three possible names for your business in the following table. Then specify the positives and negatives of each choice.

Business Name	What I Like	What I Dislike
_____	_____	_____
	_____	_____
_____	_____	_____
	_____	_____
_____	_____	_____
	_____	_____

Technology

All businesses use the Internet and technology in general to create a competitive advantage. Some businesses, such as e-businesses, are primarily Internet businesses that rely strictly on technology as a method for purchasing their product or service. Other businesses use the Internet and technology as one component of their entire business. Whichever type of business you end up starting and operating, remember that technology, and in particular the Internet, can be your most valuable asset.

Because of the Internet, businesses are getting smaller in terms of both their physical structure and human resources. The Internet, as part of an overall technology strategy, gives any entrepreneurial venture a competitive edge for a variety of reasons, including the following:

- It allows you to build sustainable size quickly and easily. Because it allows you to reach customers without spending much money, it is the perfect marketing tool.

- It encourages collaboration with virtual partners. I once worked with the Society of Home Business Owners on a project without even meeting any of the owners of the business.

- It allows customers to easily and quickly find you and what you have to offer.

- It makes it possible to manage all of your partnerships online, thus creating time for you to do what you do best.

Technology is particularly useful in sales and marketing efforts. Sales and marketing can be a time-consuming practice that will challenge both your patience and persistence. When I first started my business, I was on a very tight marketing budget and had to do a lot of the personal marketing on a shoestring budget. The Internet has made the marketing of start-up businesses much easier. Given the power of the Internet, there are millions of customers waiting to be reached and attracted to your product or service.

How can you use the technology and the Internet to help you market your business? Try the following:

- Use e-mail blasts to communicate rapidly and easily with your customers, suppliers, and collaborators around the world.

- Use desktop publishing software to develop brochures, business cards, newsletters, and other promotional materials.

- Develop a business website to sell products and services easily and inexpensively. When you develop your business website, remember to make it attractive and easy to use, keep all of the content on your pages current, create a newsletter customers can sign up to receive, make it easy for customers to purchase your product or service, and offer some type of e-commerce option.

- Blog about your industry or business to create a buzz that stimulates customer buying and establishes you as an expert in your specialty area. Through blogs, you can get in front of your potential customers many times before they even get to your website to purchase your product or service. Blogs allow you to have two-way conversations with your audience and develop a unique voice in your specific industry. You can develop free blogs at WordPress (www.wordpress.com).

- Use the power of social networking sites such as Twitter (www.twitter.com) and LinkedIn (www.linkedin.com) to drive new traffic to your website and link new sites to yours.

Choosing Your Favorite Advertising Media

Think about how you will market your product or service to prospective customers. What are your favorite types of advertising media? Check or list them below:

☐ Blogging

☐ Website with e-commerce

☐ Social networking (LinkedIn, Facebook, etc.)

☐ Direct mail marketing

☐ Television advertising

☐ Radio advertising

☐ Presentations about your product or service

☐ Word of mouth

☐ Corporate advertising for franchises

☐ Other: _____

_____

_____

Business Plan, Part 2: Your Sales and Marketing Strategy

Sales and Marketing Strategy: This section illustrates your knowledge about the specific marketing strategies you plan to use. In this section, you will map out a strategy for reaching your customers and bringing their business to you.

Marketing strategy (How will you get the message out to your potential customers?):

_____

_____

What advertising media will you use?

_____

_____

Why will this marketing strategy appeal to your customers?

_____

_____

(continued)

Business Plan, Part 2: Your Sales and Marketing Strategy (continued)

Customer Strategy: This section illustrates your knowledge about the specific industry of your business. This section includes the marketing research data you have collected, as well as the marketing strategy you will use to promote your business to your customer base. In this section, you will map out a strategy for reaching your customers and bringing their business to you.

Target market:

_____

_____

Customer profile (Who are the types of people you expect to be your customers and why?):

_____

_____

Provide any demographic statistics you have researched:

_____

_____

_____

_____

Competitor Strategy: This section illustrates your knowledge about the competitors in your specific industry. In this section, you will identify your major competitors and demonstrate that you have a full understanding of your market sector and the role your business will assume in it.

Market competitors:

_____

_____

_____

Strengths of my product in comparison with my competitors:

_____

_____

_____

Weaknesses of my product in comparison with my competitors:

_____

_____

_____

Branding Strategy: This section describes how you will develop and promote a personal brand for your business.

What is your brand name?

_____

How will you promote your brand?

_____

_____

_____

What makes your brand unique?

_____

_____

_____

(continued)

Business Plan, Part 2: Your Sales and Marketing Strategy (continued)

Technology Strategy: This section describes the technology you have available and the technology that you will need to begin and operate your business.

What technology do you currently have that you will use for your business?

_____

_____

_____

What technology do you need to begin your business?

_____

_____

_____

_____

What technology do you need to grow your business?

_____

_____

_____

_____

How will you use e-mail blasts to build your customer base?

_____

_____

_____

_____

What desktop publishing software are you using/will you use to create marketing materials?

_____

_____

_____

_____

How would you evaluate your business website's effectiveness? If you do not have a website, write the steps you need to take in order to develop one.

_____

_____

_____

_____

What do you blog about? If you do not blog, go to www.wordpress.com and begin blogging. In the space below, describe some potential topics to blog about.

_____

_____

_____

_____

What social networking sites are you registered with?

_____

_____

_____

_____

This chapter helped you develop the sales and marketing aspects of your business plan by helping you to think about the marketing strategies you will use to sell your service or product. The next chapter is designed to help you develop the organization of operations aspects of your business plan and your business.

CHAPTER 9

Organize Your
Business Operations

As entrepreneurs, we tend to be great idea people, but often we are not very organized, although there are exceptions. A fact of life for all entrepreneurs, though, is that owning a business requires some organization of operations. *Organization of operations* refers to the inner workings and infrastructure of your business. This term covers everything that happens as you execute the business, including how it operates, how the product or service gets from idea to implementation, and how you will finance your business. Organization of operations begins as soon as you start the business planning process and in many ways is at the heart of the process. In this chapter, you have an opportunity to develop this core part of your business plan.

> **NOTE**
>
> When you are starting a business, you can use all of the advice you can get. Take the time to seek out a person who can mentor you through the business start-up process. This relationship may help you to reduce the number of errors you make in your entrepreneurial venture. Refer back to Chapter 2 for more information about finding a mentor.

The Organization of Operations Scale

The organization of operations is critical to your business success. Disorganization can cause your business to fail before you even get a good start at it.

All businesses have five distinct areas that are important in creating the organization of operations aspects of a comprehensive business plan. This assessment contains 25 statements divided equally into these important areas. Read each statement and decide the extent to which the statement describes you and your business at this point in time. Then circle the appropriate number:

> 3 = Very Descriptive
>
> 2 = Somewhat Descriptive
>
> 1 = Not At All Descriptive

Ignore the Total lines below each section. They are for scoring purposes and will be used later.

This is not a test, and there are no right or wrong answers. Do not spend too much time thinking about your answers. Your initial response will be the most true for you. Be sure to respond to every statement.

	Very Descriptive	Somewhat Descriptive	Not At All Descriptive
1. I have a legal structure for my business.	3	2	1
2. I have decided where I will begin my business.	3	2	1
3. I have a written agreement with all business consultants and partners.	3	2	1
4. I have a copyright/trademark for all my products and services.	3	2	1
5. I have a legal structure for my business that ensures I take advantage of tax benefits.	3	2	1
Section 1 Total: _____			
6. I have the insurance needed for my business.	3	2	1
7. I am protected from liability for my business.	3	2	1
8. I have talked to my insurance agent about my coverage.	3	2	1
9. I have health insurance to cover me and my family.	3	2	1
10. I have a small business license.	3	2	1
Section 2 Total: _____			
11. I am great at organizing my time and energy.	3	2	1
12. I have a regular schedule for my business that I follow daily.	3	2	1

	Very Descriptive	Somewhat Descriptive	Not At All Descriptive
13. I am good at meeting deadlines for my business.	3	2	1
14. I manage the workload of my business effectively.	3	2	1
15. I am able to stay motivated and focused when business issues become difficult.	3	2	1
Section 3 Total: _____			
16. I have consulted an attorney about legal matters for my business.	3	2	1
17. I have talked with a banker about possible financing for my business.	3	2	1
18. I have consulted an accountant about bookkeeping matters.	3	2	1
19. I have talked to a mentor about my business operation.	3	2	1
20. I have talked with a financial planning professional.	3	2	1
Section 4 Total: _____			
21. My personal and professional finances are in order.	3	2	1
22. I have/will have the start-up money I need to get my business going.	3	2	1
23. I have a plan for reinvesting money back into the business.	3	2	1
24. I am good at managing my business's finances.	3	2	1
25. I have a plan for retirement.	3	2	1
Section 5 Total: _____			

Scoring

The Organization of Operations Scale provides you with information about how prepared you are to begin operating your business. Add the numbers you have circled for each of the five sections on the previous pages. Put that total on the line marked "Total" at the end of each section.

Transfer your totals for each of the five sections to the lines below:

Legal (Section 1) Total: _____

Insurance (Section 2) Total: _____

Organization and Operation (Section 3) Total: _____

Outside Professionals (Section 4) Total: _____

Finances (Section 5) Total: _____

Your score for each section will fall into one of the following ranges:

- A score of 5 to 8 indicates that this area of your organization of operations is unhealthy. You need to work at enhancing the health of your business in this area.

- A score of 9 to 11 indicates that this area of your organization of operations is somewhat healthy. However, you need to continue working to enhance the health of your business in this area.

- A score of 12 to 15 indicates that this area of your organization of operations is healthy. The activities included in this chapter will help you to be even more successful in this area.

Legal Structures for Business

Anyone who starts their own business must become familiar with the laws and regulations that govern its operation and provide some structure for operation. This section explains several general laws and regulations, but keep in mind that there are also laws and regulations that are specific to your city and state. Thus, you should consult with an attorney and an accountant before starting your venture.

One of the initial decisions you have to make when beginning a business is which type of legal/tax structure is most appropriate for the business you intend to operate. There are five basic types of structures from which you can choose. These structures include sole proprietorship, partnership, corporation, Subchapter S corporation, and limited liability company. The advantages and disadvantages of each will be discussed in the following sections to help you determine which type is most appropriate for you.

As you proceed through the following sections, keep in mind these questions:

- Will you have a business partner?
- Will you be in a business in which you have a good chance of being sued or held personally responsible for the service you provide?
- Should you incorporate?
- Do you have the money needed to incorporate?
- Have you made arrangements for bookkeeping services?
- Do you want a business that is relatively simple at the beginning?

Sole Proprietorship

This structure is perhaps the most common and the least formal of all types of businesses. You have started a sole proprietorship when you open any type of business without formalizing the structure. In this type of business, the owner does not pay him- or herself any wages. Instead, profits and losses of the business are considered as part of the owner's earnings, thus making them subject to self-employment tax.

A sole proprietorship has these advantages:

- It is simple to start and operate.
- It requires little record keeping.
- Legal ramifications and tax laws are relatively straightforward.
- There are no incorporation costs.

A sole proprietorship has these disadvantages:

- The owner is liable for debts of the business.
- The owner is liable for lawsuits against the business.
- The owner must pay taxes on any profits.

Partnership

Partnerships are formed when two or more people start a business together and decide to share the expenses and the profits. This type of business can be exciting because people with different skills and abilities can be assets to each other.

In order to avoid the risks of being the sole owner and operator of a business, entrepreneurs in partnerships are willing to sacrifice some of the autonomy that solo entrepreneurs enjoy. They may also have to share such aspects as decision making, resources, and notions about how to run a business.

> **NOTE**
>
> If you are considering forming a partnership, make sure to have a formal written agreement—drafted by a legal professional—outlining the terms of the partnership.

A partnership has these advantages:

- All partners, not just one, are liable for debts of the business.
- Profits and losses are divided among the partners.
- Partners pay taxes only on their share of the profit or loss.
- It is a relatively simple structure to form.
- Responsibilities and finances are divided among partners.

A partnership has these disadvantages:

- Income is usually subject to self-employment tax.
- It requires more documentation than a sole proprietorship.
- Partners often disagree about the operation of the business.

Corporation

Corporations are highly regulated, formal enterprises owned by shareholders and operated for the benefit of these shareholders. Because corporations are a separate legal entity, the personal assets of the owner are protected in case of financial problems or lawsuits filed against the business.

A corporation has the following advantages:

- It raises capital through the sale of stock in the company.
- Shareholders report only the income received from the corporation (as a salary or dividends).
- It—not the shareholders—is liable for business debts.
- It has many tax benefits.

A corporation has the following disadvantages:

- It requires a great deal of accounting and legal expertise to set up and operate.
- It requires incorporation costs.

Subchapter S Corporation

A Subchapter S corporation is a cross between a partnership and a corporation. Because the Subchapter S corporation is taxed in the same way as a partnership, owners can report profits and losses on their individual income tax returns.

A Subchapter S corporation has the following advantages:

- Income of the owners is not subject to self-employment tax.
- Because it is a separate legal entity, owners' personal assets are protected.

A Subchapter S corporation has the following disadvantage:

- Losses are passed on to the owners.

Limited Liability Company

A limited liability company (LLC) is a hybrid business form that draws advantages from both corporations and partnerships. The owners of an LLC are referred to as members, and the business can be the best of both worlds for business owners.

A limited liability company has the following advantages:

- Profits and losses pass through the company to its owners for tax purposes.
- Personal assets are protected from business liability.
- There is no limit to the number of owners (members).
- It is fairly simple to operate.

A limited liability corporation has the following disadvantages:

- It is recognized differently in all states.
- Legal assistance is needed to set it up.

Remember that this section is not designed to be a comprehensive review of the different types of legal structures. It is merely designed to help you begin thinking about what type of structure fits your business model best. You should consult both an attorney and an accountant to gather information before you make any business decisions.

Insurance

In this litigious world, it pays to remember that people will bring lawsuits against you and your business. Because of this fact, you need to have various types of insurance. Some of the most common types of insurance include the following:

- Health insurance
- Fire insurance
- Liability insurance
- Product liability insurance
- Professional liability insurance (insurance for your advice or recommendations)
- Vandalism insurance
- Vehicle insurance

Talk with an insurance agent to discuss what types of coverage you and your business need.

Organization and Operation

Moving from the corporate workplace to owning your own business requires you to get organized and remain organized. Operating your business as efficiently as possible also is crucial to your success. However, because you will be doing the majority of the work yourself, day-to-day running of the business can be difficult. You will encounter such distractions as personal phone calls, household responsibilities, and demands from family members. In this section, I have included several aspects of day-to-day operations that might help you to "work smarter and not harder."

Establishing a Business Location

You will need to select an area of your home to operate your business. Almost any area of your house will do depending on the type of business you plan to operate. Think about the type of business you are planning to start. Answer the following questions:

- Are you planning to start a service business?
- Will you need special tools or equipment?
- Will you need a lot of space?

On the following page, identify the place in your home or apartment which you feel is most suitable for your business. Feel free to mark several if they apply.

☐ Garage   ☐ Living Room

☐ Basement   ☐ Den

☐ Attic   ☐ Kitchen

☐ Backyard   ☐ Bedroom

☐ Workshop   ☐ Garden

☐ Library   ☐ Office Space

☐ Storefront   ☐ Warehouse

Setting Business Hours

Following are some important questions you will have to answer concerning the hours of operation for your business:

- Will you be open or available in the mornings? Evenings? Afternoons? Some combination of hours?

- Will you work in the evenings or on weekends?

- Will you keep a constant schedule or have a flexible schedule?

The answers to these questions might well depend on the type of business you operate and the types of clients you serve. In a business where you manufacture and sell things, you can set your own schedule. You can work the hours you choose and schedule this time around your family and friends. E-commerce businesses also allow you freedom to structure your workweek. Service businesses are a little different in that they require you to deal with clients or customers. You must consider these types of questions before starting a business.

Keeping Up

Working in your own business can occupy more of your time than a traditional job. Because you will primarily be working alone (or with a relatively small number of people), you will have a tremendous amount of business responsibilities to keep up with. Following are some tips that may help you to succeed in your business:

- **Follow a regular schedule.** Choose the hours during which you would like to work and stick with those hours throughout the life span of your business. Think about whether you are a "morning person" or an "evening person." The important point to remember is to choose a schedule of working hours and stick to it.

- **Motivate yourself.** Remember that you will not have a supervisor watching over you and the work you are doing; therefore, you must be able to stay on task and not be distracted. The one drawback to being an entrepreneur is that there are often many distractions. The important point to remember is to plan your work for each day and motivate yourself to stay on task.

- **Keep daily records.** By writing down and maintaining records of your daily accomplishments, work schedule, and probable income for the day, you will be able to measure your daily income and thus help to motivate yourself. In addition, this information may help you in doing the taxes for your home-based business and give you insight into how close you are to achieving your income goals.

- **Take time off.** We all need to relax. Working too much can drain the enthusiasm and energy needed to operate your business. Even if you are doing the type of work you love in your business, it is also important to engage in constructive leisure activities, be with your friends and family, and rejuvenate your energy level.

- **Control your costs.** In order to control costs in any home-based business, you need to

  - Do the majority of the work yourself.
  - Reduce your overhead costs whenever possible.
  - Keep a close eye on your daily, monthly, and yearly costs.
  - Be sure you are paying the best price possible—shop around!
  - Keep accurate records of all your business expenses.

Outside Professionals

As a new business owner, you need to begin establishing relationships with trained and experienced outside professionals such as the following:

- **Attorney:** You will need someone to help you determine your legal structure, review your agreements and contracts, and provide legal advice.

- **Accountant:** You will need someone to help you set up a bookkeeping system for your business, as well as provide tax information.

- **Banker:** You will need someone to help provide you with sound financial information as well as a method for obtaining financing for your business.

- **Insurance agent:** You will need someone to help provide you with advice about the types and amount of coverage that are best for you and your business.

- **Mentors:** You will need people to help guide you through the start-up and operation of your business. These mentors can be entrepreneurs in your community, entrepreneur assistance sites online, or SCORE mentors (www.score.org).

The relationships that you develop prior to, and during, your business ownership can be critical and of tremendous benefit to your business.

Finances

It takes money to own and operate any kind of business. You will need money to purchase inventory, develop your product or service, create a website, and develop and implement a marketing plan.

The good news is that most businesses can be started with a minimal amount of money. Ways in which you can reduce your start-up costs include:

- Do most of the work yourself.
- Control your spending.
- Put in time rather than money.
- Work as much as you possibly can.
- Get free publicity when possible.
- Keep your overhead as low as possible.

Figuring Out Initial Costs

How much will it cost you to start your business? Check off the items that you will need to start the type of business in which you are interested and fill in the amount that each item costs.

_____ Business registration (city, state): $ _____

_____ Cost of incorporation: $ _____

_____ Licensing fee/permits required: $ _____

_____ Business checking account: $ _____

_____ Mailing supplies (stamps, envelopes, etc.): $ _____

_____ Paper and other office supplies: $ _____

_____ Professional printing: $ _____

_____ Products/materials: $ _____

_____ Advertising/promotion: $ _____

_____ Accountant's fees: $ _____

_____ Attorney's fees: $ _____

_____ Equipment: $ _____

_____ Deposits paid: $ _____

To determine the start-up and operating expenses required to start your business, complete the following worksheet.

_____Insurance fees: $ _____

_____Other: $ _____

Total estimated start-up cost: $ _____

One of the biggest concerns for people starting and operating their own business is where to get the money they need to start their business. Many entrepreneurs first turn to their own assets and savings. To evaluate how much money you have available to put into the business, complete the following worksheet.

Assessing Your Personal Finances

This worksheet is designed to help you determine the amount of money you have on hand for your business based on your current financial worth.

Assets

Cash in savings: $ _____

Cash in checking: $ _____

Certificates of deposit: $ _____

U.S. Treasury notes: $_____

Stocks and bonds: $ _____

Real estate: $ _____

Insurance: $ _____

IRAs: $ _____

Pension plans: $ _____

(continued)

Assessing Your Personal Finances (continued)

Assets (continued)

Rental property: $ _____

Other: $ _____

Total Assets: $ _____

Liabilities

Loans: $ _____

Mortgage/rental payments: $ _____

Car payments: $ _____

Child care: $ _____

Groceries: $ _____

Medical expenses: $ _____

Monthly utilities: $ _____

Taxes owed: $ _____

Other: $ _____

Total Liabilities: $ _____

Total Assets ($_____) − Total Liabilities ($_____) =

Net Worth $ _____

Without a doubt, one of the most important aspects of your finances is your cash flow. Your net worth is the amount of money you have to put in your business or your net change in cash flow for the month. Because everyone's situation is different, it is nearly impossible to determine how much net worth is needed to start your business. Many factors go into determining "the magic number" you need to finance your business, including the type of business you are planning to start, your family situation, and the structure of your business. Remember that you may be able to reduce some of your monthly liabilities, but be careful to keep enough money available to live comfortably while starting your business.

If your personal assets won't cover your start-up costs, there are other sources for financing:

- Banks and credit unions
- Home equity line of credit
- Loans
- Seed money from local economic development centers
- Micro loans from the Small Business Administration

It's important to talk to a financial professional about your business financing options.

Business Plan Final Touches

This section will help you take the information you have completed in this chapter and put it into your business plan. When you have completed the following worksheet, you will have a comprehensive business plan for your business.

Business Plan, Part 3: Your Organization of Operations

Operational Plan: The operational plan is an essential part of your business plan. It can function as the opening to your business plan and presents an overview of your business in a condensed form. Because the operational plan requires you to have a clear picture of your business, it provides the reader with a snapshot of your entire business concept.

Legal: This section describes the legal structure you have in place to offer your product or service.

_____

_____

_____

_____

Insurance: In the space below, list the various types of insurance that you still need to begin your business.

_____

_____

_____

_____

(continued)

Business Plan, Part 3:
Your Organization of Operations (continued)

Organization and Operation: This section includes your organization's structure and details about the ownership and operation of business, as well as the structure of the management team.

How will your business deliver goods or perform services?

_____

_____

What are any unique manufacturing requirements?

_____

_____

What space requirements do you have?

_____

_____

Will you use any innovative methods for delivering your product/service to your customers?

_____

_____

What are your strategies for growth?

_____

_____

Where will you operate your business from?

_____

_____

Outside Professionals: This section describes the various types of outside professionals you have consulted or plan to consult in the operation of your business.

Who have you consulted so far? What services have they provided?

_____

_____

Who do you still need to consult? What services will they provide for you?

_____

_____

Finances: This section describes the amount of funding you will need to start or expand your business. As an entrepreneur, you should always remember that sales numbers drive your business.

What capital is required for your business start-up?

_____

_____

What personal funds will you use for your business?

_____

_____

How much will you charge?

_____

_____

How much will you make per transaction?

_____

_____

Personal financial status:

_____

_____

(continued)

Business Plan, Part 3:
Your Organization of Operations (continued)

Other: This section provides space for you to address any other issues that are important in getting your business off the ground.

_____

_____

_____

_____

_____

_____

In the last three chapters, you have had the opportunity to develop various aspects of your business and put together a comprehensive business plan that will guide the development growth of your business. By having a business plan, you have identified both the strengths and the potential weaknesses of your business. Part 4 is designed to help you develop critical skills needed to cope with the ups and downs of being an entrepreneur.

Part 4: Developing Entrepreneurial Skills

"Though entrepreneurship may offer the occasional act of swashbuckling derring-do—or, at least, high points of excitement—business owners usually just have to move forward through a not very glamorous, prolonged state of pulse-pounding tension about whether their business will make it."

—Joe Robinson

CHAPTER 10

Manage Your Money

One of the things that keeps people from succeeding in their own businesses is the management of personal and business finances. Personal finances and business finances are linked, and entrepreneurs need to be prepared to manage their money in both areas.

As you strive to turn your business idea into a profitable business, you will ask yourself the following questions:

- Do I have enough money to begin the business?
- How will I financially keep the business operating?
- When am I making enough money to quit my job?
- Do I have enough money to create a product or service to provide?
- Do I have enough money to live on while the business becomes viable?
- How do I handle my personal money and my business money?

The answer to these and many other questions you have about money can be answered by identifying your money management style. Money management encompasses how you handle money, how you keep track of profits and losses, and what you do with the money you make in the business. Your individual money management style is your preferred method of dealing with money on a day-to-day basis. This style is a result of your fears, goals, childhood upbringing, education, and emotions related to spending and saving money. Managing your money and developing a financial plan can be difficult if you do not understand yourself and your money style.

Beginning your business without a firm grasp on your money management style and your ability to harness your financial resources can be risky. The Money Management Style Inventory that follows will help you to identify your money management style and then help you to explore the origins, strengths, and weaknesses of this style. When you are aware of who you are and what your money management style is, you will be better able to use your current money management style to the fullest and develop the skills you are lacking so that you can better manage your money and develop a financial plan that fits your personality.

The Money Management Style Inventory

People have a lot of different emotions about money. They love it, worship it, fear it, hate it, don't understand it, or simply accept it for what it is. And for many people, managing the money they earn is often a problem.

People use different money management styles based on their personality characteristics, yet most people fall into one of five distinct behavior patterns. They view money as something to be spent on pleasurable items and activities, something to be saved, something to be hoarded, something to amass into a fortune, or something to be risked.

The Money Management Style Inventory (MMSI) can help you identify—based on your personality—your approach in spending and saving money. This quiz contains 50 statements. Read each statement and decide whether it describes you. If the statement does describe you, circle the words *Like Me*. If, on the other hand, the statement does not describe you, circle the words *Not Like Me*.

This is not a test. There are no right or wrong answers, so do not spend too much time thinking about your answers. Be sure to respond to every statement.

1. I buy whatever brings me pleasure.	Like Me	Not Like Me
2. I often buy gifts for other people.	Like Me	Not Like Me
3. I have a hard time in budgeting my money.	Like Me	Not Like Me
4. Saving money is difficult for me.	Like Me	Not Like Me
5. I buy things on impulse.	Like Me	Not Like Me
6. I often overspend.	Like Me	Not Like Me
7. I am often in debt.	Like Me	Not Like Me
8. I am not afraid to spend all the money I have.	Like Me	Not Like Me
9. No gift is priced too high for me.	Like Me	Not Like Me
10. I get a thrill from buying things.	Like Me	Not Like Me
Section 1 Total: _____		
11. I like to hold onto my money.	Like Me	Not Like Me
12. I am great at saving money.	Like Me	Not Like Me

13. I have a budget that I stick to.	Like Me	Not Like Me
14. I do not buy nonessential items.	Like Me	Not Like Me
15. I buy only what I need.	Like Me	Not Like Me
16. I am focused on financial stability.	Like Me	Not Like Me
17. I like the security of having money in the bank.	Like Me	Not Like Me
18. I usually pay cash for my purchases.	Like Me	Not Like Me
19. I am rarely in credit-card debt.	Like Me	Not Like Me
20. I save at least 10 percent of my salary every month.	Like Me	Not Like Me

Section 2 Total: _____

21. I often worry about my finances.	Like Me	Not Like Me
22. I feel like it is up to me to control my money.	Like Me	Not Like Me
23. I check my financial account balances often.	Like Me	Not Like Me
24. I often think about what might happen to my money.	Like Me	Not Like Me
25. If I just had more money, I could stop worrying about it.	Like Me	Not Like Me
26. I worry that I will not have enough retirement savings.	Like Me	Not Like Me
27. I like my money in safe investments.	Like Me	Not Like Me
28. I like to be able to get my hands on my money easily.	Like Me	Not Like Me
29. I worry when I make a major purchase.	Like Me	Not Like Me
30. I spend a lot of emotional energy worrying about finances.	Like Me	Not Like Me

Section 3 Total: _____

31. I want to achieve great wealth.	Like Me	Not Like Me
32. I believe that with wealth comes power and status.	Like Me	Not Like Me
33. I put a lot of time into managing my money.	Like Me	Not Like Me
34. I often spend hours hunting for the best investments.	Like Me	Not Like Me
35. I use a personal finance computer program.	Like Me	Not Like Me
36. I like to occasionally flaunt my wealth.	Like Me	Not Like Me
37. I think that having a lot of money impresses people.	Like Me	Not Like Me
38. I get obsessed with tracking my money.	Like Me	Not Like Me
39. My self-worth comes from my investment portfolio.	Like Me	Not Like Me
40. I often shift investments to get the best returns.	Like Me	Not Like Me

Section 4 Total: _____

41. I enjoy taking risks with money.	Like Me	Not Like Me
42. I am competitive when it comes to money.	Like Me	Not Like Me
43. I get a rush from intense experience.	Like Me	Not Like Me
44. I like the adrenaline rush from risking my money.	Like Me	Not Like Me
45. I play the lottery regularly.	Like Me	Not Like Me
46. I thrive on uncertainty.	Like Me	Not Like Me
47. I always go for broke with my money.	Like Me	Not Like Me

(continued)

(continued)

48. Others say I am too aggressive in my investments.	Like Me	Not Like Me
49. If I lose money, I believe more will come my way.	Like Me	Not Like Me
50. I am motivated by variety and change.	Like Me	Not Like Me
Section 5 Total: _____		

Scoring

The Money Management Style Inventory (MMSI) is designed to measure your money management style. To score the MMSI, add the number of Like Me responses you circled in each of the five previous sections. Then transfer your totals for each of the five sections to the corresponding lines below:

> Spenders (Section 1) Total: _____
>
> Savers (Section 2) Total: _____
>
> Hoarders (Section 3) Total: _____
>
> Amassers (Section 4) Total: _____
>
> Risk Takers (Section 5) Total: _____

The area in which you scored the highest tends to be your most preferred money management style. Similarly, the area in which you scored the lowest tends to be your least preferred style for managing your money. Be sure to read the following section that describes your preferred money management style. If you had the same score for several of the styles, read each of them and decide which money management style fits you most, or think about how you can combine the two styles in managing your money.

Spenders

As an entrepreneurial Spender, you are not afraid to spend money to make your business successful. In fact, you probably feel that spending money on your business is the way to ensure its success. You may even buy things you do not need, as long as you think it will help the chances of your business being successful. You often feel compelled to spend or charge money easily and quickly for your business, even if you can't afford the purchases. You believe that you will make the money back by selling your product or service.

In your daily life, you tend to get carried away by instant gratification. You often find it difficult to think about anything else other than spending your money. You are likely to have many credit cards, and many of them are probably charged to their limit.

As a Spender, you tend to fit the following characteristics:

- You are prone to frequently get overdue notices for bills past due.
- You overspend to feel better about your business chances.
- Spending can be a form of addiction for you.

- You often delude yourself about why you keep buying things for your business.
- You feel like you will be happier if you purchase material things for your business.
- You have revolving debt on your credit cards.

Spender's Questions for Reflection

How do you attempt to hide your tendency to overspend money?

_____

_____

How many times do you break your budget by spending more than you make? How can you fix this situation?

_____

_____

What do you think causes you to overspend on your business?

_____

_____

What do you think are the deep-seated roots to your overspending?

_____

_____

What effect have your childhood and your parents' spending habits had on you?

_____

_____

How does spending money make you feel?

_____

_____

What types of activities could you engage in to get the same pleasure you get from spending money?

_____

_____

As a Spender, you may want to try some of the following techniques:

- Work closely with your financial planner to develop a fiscal responsibility program for your business.
- The next time you want to make a large purchase, wait until the next day. If you still feel like you need the purchase, go ahead and buy it.
- Think about ways that you can work on your business to improve it without spending money.

Savers

As an entrepreneurial Saver, you tend to be financially stable. You feel a sense of pride in how you make and manage the money you will use for your business. You focus primarily on feeling safe and secure and running your business in a way to ensure that you stay that way. Your debts tend to be under control and you will probably not feel the need to go in debt to start and operate your business. You frequently check your total personal and business assets so that you will feel more psychologically and economically secure.

As a Saver, you tend to fit the following characteristics:

- When it comes to money, you are organized and focused on stability.
- You tend to be educated about money and financial planning strategies for your personal and business finances.
- You have conservative spending habits about your personal and business finances.
- You do not like change of any kind.
- You believe that the way to financial security is through steady, conservative investments.
- You enjoy planning for your business success.

Saver's Questions for Reflection

How are your spending and saving habits similar to or different from those of your parents?

_____

_____

What would you do if you won one million dollars in the lottery? How would you manage the money?

_____

_____

What types of materials about financial planning do you read?

_____

_____

In what ways do you feel you live below your means?

_____

_____

Do your spending and saving habits ever cause conflict between you and significant others? In what ways?

_____

_____

What risk would you like to take with your money that you have been afraid to take in the past?

_____

_____

As a Saver, you may want to try some of the following techniques:

- Work closely with your financial planner to develop a plan for spending money on your business when it is needed.
- Don't allow your insecurities about finances affect your ability to make your business grow.
- Take calculated risks with the money you are spending on your business.

Hoarders

As an entrepreneurial Hoarder, you tend to believe that the only way to feel financially secure is to hang on to every penny you earn. You worry about money and often let your anxiety get in the way of the success of your business. You prefer thrift over spending and are frugal when it comes to reinvesting money back into your business. You are terribly afraid of losing your money, and you want to be prepared for long periods of business inactivity or downturns in the economy.

As a Hoarder, you tend to fit the following characteristics:

- You build a stash of money that you can fall back on in case you need it for your business.
- You like budgeting your money and live by a tight monthly personal and business budget.
- You like comparison shopping for the best deals when you shop for your business.
- You are disciplined about money and are not influenced by advertisements or sales.
- You definitely live within your monetary means.
- You keep a balanced checkbook.

Hoarder's Questions for Reflection

What risks would you like to begin taking with your money?

_____

_____

How could you better enjoy your money now?

_____

_____

What is your greatest fear related to spending and saving money? Why do you have this fear?

_____

_____

How does being financially comfortable feel to you?

_____

_____

What types of personal and business financial disasters do you fear?

_____

_____

Is there a particular incident in your life that made you afraid of losing your money?

_____

_____

Has your life, or the life of your family, suffered because you do not spend money on things you can afford?

_____

_____

In what ways do you think you might be too safe with your money? How will this affect your business?

_____

_____

As a Hoarder, you may want to focus on the following points:

- Understand that a certain amount of profits needs to go back into the business if it is to succeed and grow.
- Think about small risks you can take with your business profits and and how you can build on the results.
- Don't let your fears keep you from building the business that you desire.

Amassers

As an entrepreneurial Amasser, you view money as status and live as if you make more money than you really do. You use profits from your business to keep score and compare yourself with others. You like to keep up with and surpass the "Joneses." You feel like the more you have, the more successful you are. Therefore, your worth is tied to your possessions and the value of your business. Buying upscale materials and goods enhances the feelings you have about your business. You may purchase nice cars, homes, and clothes, but you probably do not have an emergency fund set aside for hard times. You may not even realize how much money you are spending, as opposed to saving or investing in your business.

As an Amasser, you tend to fit the following characteristics:

- You probably have the drive and energy to make a lot of money from your business.
- You are willing to work hard, and you take great pride in your business accomplishments.
- You are a natural achiever and enjoy spending money as a symbol of your achievements.
- You think that appearances are important, and you usually have the nicest things in order to keep up appearances.
- You tend to overestimate how much you earn and underestimate how much you spend personally and on your business.

- When you see things you want, you go ahead and buy them regardless of how much they cost.
- You often put yourself and your business venture in financial jeopardy so that you can purchase upscale possessions.
- You often find yourself driven to purchase things you cannot afford.

Amasser's Questions for Reflection

How will your work ethic affect the operation of your business?

_____

_____

What do you spend money on most?

_____

_____

What types of things do you buy that you might not be able to afford while your business gets off the ground?

_____

_____

How will your spending habits change when you start a business?

_____

_____

As an Amasser, you may want to try some of the following techniques:

- Set goals that are right for you and your business. Don't try and keep up with others.

- Set aside some of the money you make in your business for when sales are low.

- Put some of the money you earn in your business back into the business to ensure continued growth.

Risk Takers

As an entrepreneurial Risk Taker, you believe that the only way to get what you want in your business is to take significant risks. You always want whatever is bigger and greater in your business ventures. You get an emotional rush from gambling on financial hunches. You trust your instincts that your risks will pay off.

As a Risk Taker, you tend to fit the following characteristics:

- You always go for broke with your money.

- You tend to be charismatic and creative in earning and spending money from your business.

- You don't mind unpredictability and uncertainty when it comes to managing your money.

- You will gamble on your own ability to make a lot of money from your business.

- If you do invest your money, you probably will invest in the highest-risk business ventures.

Risk Taker's Questions for Reflection

What types of risks do you tend to take most often?

_____

_____

What types of risks do you need to take more often?

_____

_____

Are there risks you should not continue to take?

_____

_____

What surprises you about your risk-taking abilities?

_____

_____

(continued)

Risk Taker's Questions for Reflection (continued)

Do the risks you take reflect what matters most to you?

_____

_____

Are you taking the amount of risks you feel you should be taking? Why or why not?

_____

_____

Are you taking the types of risks you feel you should be taking? Why or why not?

_____

_____

Are you taking too many foolish risks? Describe these risks.

_____

_____

What types of risks do you tend to avoid? Why?

_____

_____

As a Risk Taker, you may want to try some of the following techniques:

- Talk with your financial planner about risky money transactions you plan to make.

- Back up your hunches with facts by completing research before you take a risk.

- Reflect on and re-evaluate the risks you do take so that you will avoid the foolish ones and act on the necessary ones in the future.

Your Financial Management Plan

Handling personal finances and the finances of a business is fraught with risk, and financial risks can be stressful for any entrepreneur. Entrepreneurs must tolerate a certain amount of debt and its consequences, including the potential loss of savings or a home, a decrease in income from employment, repayment of various types of loans, and credit-card debt. Mounting debt and dwindling business gains can cause the most confident entrepreneurs to question their reasons for starting a business.

Financially related stress can be so powerful that you may begin to question your dream. To maintain your confidence and sense of control, you will need a personal financial management plan that is comparable to your business plan. Following are some tools and techniques that will help you manage your money more effectively.

In Chapter 9, you completed a worksheet that helped you examine your assets and liabilities to ensure that you had sufficient funds for starting your business. The worksheet that follows will help you to determine whether you have the sufficient monthly cash flow to maintain and grow your business by providing you with valuable data about how much you spend per month.

Tracking Monthly Expenses

You (and your family) will need to begin keeping track of your spending. The best way to do this is to get a notepad and write down those things that you spend money on. After you have done this for a few days, you will begin to understand your daily spending habits. Becoming aware of the monthly fixed costs and expenses is a great starting point to managing your money. This worksheet is designed to help you determine the approximate amount of money you will have to operate your business.

Housing and Utilities

Rent or mortgage: $ _____

Homeowner's insurance: $ _____

Homeowner's association dues: $ _____

Property taxes: $ _____

Household repairs: $ _____

Gas and electricity: $ _____

Water and sewage: $ _____

Trash: $ _____

Other: $ _____

Housing and Utilities Total: $ _____

(continued)

Tracking Monthly Expenses (continued)

Living

Food and beverages: $ _____

Medical/dental insurance: $ _____

Prescriptions and other health expenses: $ _____

Life insurance: $ _____

Clothing: $ _____

Education: $ _____

Entertainment: $ _____

Child care: $ _____

Telephone: $ _____

TV/cable/satellite: $ _____

Internet: $ _____

Personal grooming: $ _____

Memberships: $ _____

Pet care: $ _____

Other: $ _____

Living Total: $ _____

Debt

Credit card payments: $ _____

Student loan repayment: $ _____

Personal loan repayment: $ _____

Other debt payment: $ _____

Debt Total: $ _____

Transportation

Car loan payment: $ _____

Car insurance: $ _____

Parking: $ _____

Gas: $ _____

Car repairs: $ _____

Public transit: $_____

Other: $ _____

Transportation Total: $ _____

Monthly Expenses Total: $ _____

(Total of Housing, Living, Debt, and Transportation sections)

Household Income

Monthly take-home pay: $ _____

Monthly take-home pay (significant other): $ _____

Other/Business income: $ _____

Monthly Household Income Total: $ _____

(continued)

Tracking Monthly Expenses (continued)

To calculate your monthly net cash flow, complete the following equation:

$\quad$ \$ _____ (Monthly Household Income)

$-$ \$ _____ (Monthly Expenses)

$=$ \$ _____ (Net Cash Flow)

Now that you see where your money is going each month and have determined your net cash flow, it's time to make decisions about the adjustments you need to make to have enough money for your business and personal expenses. Keep in mind that in order to ensure the success of your business, you need to have a savings cushion for household expenses in addition to the money you need to support and reinvest into your business.

To build this cushion, you will need to get control over your spending habits. If you feel like your net cash flow is a sufficient amount of money (called positive cash flow) to meet your expenses and provide this cushion, you will not need to make many (if any) changes. If, however, the amount is not sufficient (called negative cash flow), you need to think about ways that you can cut your spending. For some money management styles, this task will be easier than for others. Note that if you have a significant other, you will need to discuss your money management ideas with that person.

To reduce your spending and bring your cash flow back into balance, look at your monthly spending in specific categories (such as clothing, education, entertainment). Do any of these stand out as being unnecessarily large amounts? If so, take a snapshot of your spending behavior in this area by answering these questions:

- How much do you spend on regular routine purchases?
- How much do you spend on impulse versus what you need?
- What feelings trigger the desire to purchase the items?

Another strategy is to evaluate regular expenses and eliminate those that aren't essential. The Examining Monthly Luxuries worksheet provides an opportunity to do this. In the last worksheet in this chapter, you can use what you have learned about your money management style and monthly expenses to come up with specific actions that will best fit your situation.

Examining Monthly Luxuries

This exercise is designed to help you separate necessities from luxuries in your life. Complete the sections below by listing your monthly luxuries in the right-hand column. What themes do you see?

Area	*Luxuries*
Home	_____
	_____
Food/beverage	_____
	_____
Clothing	_____
	_____
Education	_____
	_____
Entertainment	_____
	_____
Child-related expenses	_____
	_____
Transportation	_____
	_____
Personal care	_____
	_____
Spouse/partner expenses	_____
	_____

(continued)

Examining Monthly Luxuries (continued)

Limiting Your Spending

In the spaces below, list some of the things you can do today to begin limiting your overspending. Some suggestions might include cutting up your credit cards, developing a financial plan, seeing a financial planner, and paying off your outstanding debts.

_____

_____

_____

_____

_____

_____

_____

This chapter has helped you to identify your money management style so that you can manage your money while you are starting and operating your business. Remember that as an entrepreneur you do not earn money consistently. It will be critical (especially in the start-up stage of your business) that you develop skills in managing your personal money and the money you make in your business. The next chapter will help you manage your time while operating your business.

CHAPTER 11

Manage Your Time

One of the leading causes of stress for entrepreneurs is that they have too much to do and not enough time to do it. In the fast-paced world of entrepreneurism, learning how to manage time well can help to alleviate stress and increase success. For those entrepreneurs who are managed by time, time brings anxiety, exhaustion, and complication. For entrepreneurs who are instead good time managers, time brings satisfaction, relaxation, and productivity.

In this chapter, you will assess your current time management skills in five different areas. Then you will work through several exercises to improve the way you manage your time.

Risk-Taking Paralysis

Many people dream of starting their own business, but not many know how to manage their time well enough to turn their dream into a reality. Often thoughts of entrepreneurial dreams and goals are accompanied by feelings of frustration. These dreams and goals seem to be too far into the future to reach and to require too much time to achieve.

If you are like other entrepreneurs, you feel like you just don't have enough time to do everything that needs doing. The gap between where you are now and where you want to be—in a business of your very own—may seem wide. In reality, one of the biggest barriers that may be keeping you from launching your own entrepreneurial venture is the mental paralysis that keeps you from taking a chance.

You have a great idea and a masterful marketing plan, with some money saved on the side to build a website and get thousands of customers. However, something keeps you from pulling the trigger and starting your own business. Little doubts begin to creep into your thinking, and you say such things to yourself as "The time's not right, I will begin next month" and "Maybe I should tweak my idea a little" or "This idea probably isn't good enough to work."

I know exactly how you are feeling right now—I've been there. These negative thoughts that keep streaming through your head at this juncture of the entrepreneurial process are natural and are experienced by most entrepreneurs. They are your mind's way of trying to protect you from doing something you might regret. However, these negative thoughts become behavioral factors (see Figure 11.1) that paralyze you from taking action to begin your business or grow your business. The Time Management Scale will help you recognize whether these factors are affecting your ability to move ahead in your business.

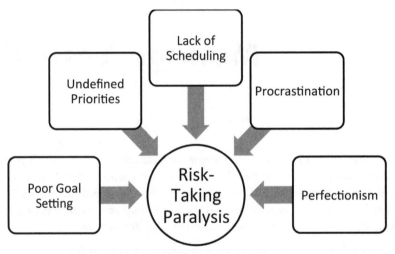

Figure 11.1: The factors in risk-taking paralysis.

Symptoms of Poor Time Management

Entrepreneurs tend to be poor time managers for a variety of reasons, including a lack of a distraction-free space for operating their business, an inability to prioritize their projects and workload, and an inability to maintain a structured schedule. Here are the signs that you may need to develop better time management skills:

- Forgetfulness
- Difficulty concentrating on things

- Tired a lot of the time
- Feeling overwhelmed
- Juggling activities and priorities
- Sleeplessness
- Irritability
- Headaches
- Lack of life enjoyment

The Time Management Scale

The Time Management Scale contains 40 statements that are related to your time management skills. Read each of the statements and decide whether the statement describes you. If the statement *does* describe you, circle the number in the Yes column next to that item. If the statement does *not* describe you, circle the number in the No column next to that item. Your initial response will likely be the most true for you. Be sure to respond to every statement.

	Yes	No
1. I have written down my short-term goals.	2	1
2. I rarely write down my business plans for the future.	1	2
3. I use goal setting strategies to decide what to work on next.	2	1
4. I stress out about business deadlines.	1	2
5. I have no long-term business goals to keep me motivated.	1	2
6. Before I complete a task, I make sure the results are worth the time.	2	1
7. I often set and work toward unattainable goals.	1	2
8. I take on more commitments than I have time to complete.	1	2
Section 1 Total: _____		
9. I hang on to mail and e-mail messages even though I know they are unimportant.	1	2
10. When I work on tasks, I start with those of the highest priority.	2	1
11. I know how much time I spend on the business-related tasks I do.	2	1
12. I analyze new tasks for their importance and then prioritize them.	2	1

(continued)

(continued)

	Yes	No
13. I keep a prioritized to-do list.	2	1
14. I talk to my mentors and significant others about the priorities of tasks I am given.	2	1
15. I hate to delegate jobs even though I know I cannot complete them.	1	2
16. I work on projects that will yield the best results.	2	1

Section 2 Total: _____

	Yes	No
17. People say that I "have no sense of time."	1	2
18. I have a daily planner I use in my business.	2	1
19. I have a filing system for business papers.	2	1
20. I set time aside to make plans for my business.	2	1
21. I check my to-do list regularly for new tasks.	2	1
22. I have time built into my schedule to deal with unexpected events.	2	1
23. I feel lost without a watch.	2	1
24. I am often late.	1	2

Section 3 Total: _____

	Yes	No
25. I complete most business projects at the last minute.	1	2
26. I put off tasks that may be too difficult.	1	2
27. I often put off things because I am afraid of making mistakes.	1	2
28. I have trouble achieving deadlines set for me.	1	2
29. I have difficulty getting started on new projects or transitioning from one project to the next.	1	2
30. I try to return phone calls and e-mails within 24 hours.	2	1
31. I rarely have to ask for more time to meet business deadlines.	2	1
32. I procrastinate a lot.	1	2

Section 4 Total: _____

	Yes	No
33. I never do anything halfway—it's all or nothing.	1	2
34. The thought of making a mistake angers me.	1	2
35. People say I expect too much of myself and my business.	1	2
36. I feel down or empty even when I accomplish something.	1	2
37. No matter how much I've done, there's always more I could do.	1	2
38. I try not to criticize myself and others too excessively.	2	1
39. I feel humiliated when things aren't perfect.	1	2
40. I am not afraid to make mistakes—that's how I learn.	2	1

Section 5 Total: _____

Scoring

Add each of the five Yes columns and write the numbers in the blank spaces below.

Goal Setting (Section 1): _____

Prioritizing (Section 2): _____

Scheduling (Section 3): _____

Procrastination (Section 4): _____

Perfectionism (Section 5): _____

A score from 14 to 16 indicates that you tend to have effective time management skills in this area. A score from 11 to 13 indicates that you have adequate time management skills in this area, but there is room for improvement. A score from 8 to 10 indicates that you have limited time management skills in this area. You need to do as much as possible to enhance your time management skills for personal and professional growth.

If you are struggling with time management, don't worry—you're not alone. Many entrepreneurs feel that there is not enough time in the day and that they need to practice effective time management skills. The following sections include exercises for each of the areas on the Time Management Scale. Regardless of how you scored on each of the areas, you will benefit from these time-management exercises. By learning better time management skills, you can regain control over your life and your business. Rather than getting bogged down and not getting enough done, you can choose what you need to work on and when to work on it.

Goal Setting

Determining exactly what you would like to see happen in your business in the future is important. For example, you may want to increase your marketing efforts, hire additional help, incorporate your business, or apply for a patent. Having such goals will help to give order and context to your daily schedule because you will need to give both time and energy to these goals in order to achieve them. Without effective goal setting, you are likely to spend your time on conflicting priorities. By setting goals, you will save yourself time, effort, and frustration in the future. Once you have set goals, you know where you are going and what you need to do to get there.

The first step in setting and reaching effective goals is to define them so they are realistic and achievable. Take a look at some sample goals:

- "Be successful."
- "Make a lot of money."
- "Write a book."
- "Be a good leader."
- "Be a better salesperson."

Notice that these goals are vague and difficult to measure. In contrast, effective goals are SMART:

- **Specific:** Goals must be stated in concrete, behavioral terms. For example, "increase business sales by 10 percent next month" is a concrete, behavioral goal.

- **Measurable:** Goals must be measurable so that you can track your progress. For example, you would be able to determine whether your sales increase by 10 percent next month.

- **Attainable:** Goals must be within your reach, or you will not be motivated to work toward them. You must feel like you have a realistic opportunity to achieve your goals. For example, you might feel like you have created enough contacts to sell 15 more products next month to meet your goal.

- **Relevant:** Goals must be important to you. For example, knowing that the sales of a product is the primary way you generate income, so increasing sales numbers will ensure the success of your business.

- **Timed:** Goals must have deadlines attached to them if they are going to motivate you, though you need to be reasonable and set deadlines that you can realistically commit to. For example, by stating that you will increase sales next month, you are giving yourself a deadline to achieve the goal. This deadline will enhance your motivation and prevent you from procrastinating.

Defining Your Goals

Define your own goals. They should be positively stated and realistic, identify specific behaviors, and be within your ability to achieve. Use the space below to set up to five goals that will help you to build your business. These goals can be related to any aspect of your business.

1. I will . . . _____

_____

2. I will . . . _____

_____

3. I will . . . _____

_____

4. I will . . . _____

_____

5. I will . . . _____

_____

Prioritizing

You need to develop a system for prioritizing and adding structure to your work. To work effectively, you need to work on the tasks that have the highest value and importance. Prioritizing is your ability to see the various tasks that are important and give those tasks more of your time, energy, and attention. In prioritizing, you focus on what is important and needs to be done most urgently, and then you move on to less urgent tasks.

Establishing Short-Range and Long-Range Goals

The next step is to prioritize the goals you identified into long-term and short-term goals by importance. Short-term goals are objectives that you would like to achieve in a year or less. These goals may be changed or revised as new options present themselves. Long-term goals are objectives that you want to achieve over a longer period of time, such as one to five years into the future. Try to clarify what is urgent, what is somewhat important, and what can wait until later.

Ranking Your Goals

Look at your list of business goals from the previous worksheet and determine which are long-term and which are short-term. Then consider which of these goals is most important to you. Write the goals in the appropriate columns below, starting with the most important.

Long-Term Goals	*Short-Term Goals*
_____	_____
_____	_____
_____	_____
_____	_____
_____	_____

Using To-Do Lists

To-do lists can help you both to identify tasks and assignments that need to be completed and to motivate you to remember them and work toward accomplishing them. Making to-do lists eventually becomes a habit that can help you remain organized in your business. To begin with, think about important things you need to do tomorrow and complete the Daily Planning worksheet. When you have completed a daily to-do list, you can work on one for the upcoming week.

Daily Planning

In the following columns, list the tasks you need to complete, phone calls you need to make to people, and appointments you need to keep. As you complete the tasks, place a check mark in the Completed column.

Time	Tasks	Phone Calls	Appointments	Completed
7 a.m.				
8 a.m.				
9 a.m.				
10 a.m.				
11 a.m.				
12 noon				
1 p.m.				
2 p.m.				
3 p.m.				
4 p.m.				
5 p.m.				

Time	Tasks	Phone Calls	Appointments	Completed
6 p.m.	_____	_____	_____	_____
	_____	_____	_____	_____
7 p.m.	_____	_____	_____	_____
	_____	_____	_____	_____

Weekly Planning

In the list below, think about your next week and identify and write down some of the many things that you need to accomplish. Be as comprehensive as possible.

Things I Need to Do This Week

Monday _____

_____

Tuesday _____

_____

Wednesday _____

_____

Thursday _____

_____

Friday _____

_____

Saturday _____

_____

Sunday _____

_____

Take your weekly to-do list and prioritize it, using the following steps:

1. Break your list down based on time limits you face. Those tasks that are most important should be prioritized to the top of your weekly to-do list.

2. Think about the consequences that will occur if you are unable to complete something on your to-do list. Do this with every item on your list to determine which items can be considered top priority on your list.

3. Think about the tasks that are not very important and move those to the bottom of your priority list.

Using this process of prioritizing can help you become more organized and more efficient. The Setting Priorities worksheet provides an opportunity for you to put this process into practice by listing your weekly goals in order of importance.

Setting Priorities

In the following form, list your tasks for next week based on their priority. In the first column, list high- and low-priority tasks. Place a check mark once you have completed the tasks, and write "yes" or "no" based on whether follow-up is needed.

High-Priority Tasks	Completed	Follow-Up?

Low-Priority Tasks	Completed	Follow-Up?

Scheduling

Scheduling is the process of allocating time for prioritized goals. It is allowing yourself time to both accomplish individual goals and handle unexpected events and interruptions. You need to begin creating a schedule that can help to keep you on track and protect you from procrastination and the stress that goes with it.

Following are some techniques that may help you in scheduling your time more effectively:

- **Block out your time.** Set aside several hours each day to spend toward accomplishing one of your goals. When would you like to block out time during your day?

- **Break large goals into many smaller goals.** What large goal do you have that you would like to break down into smaller goals?

Strive to provide a set time schedule to achieve goals rather than having it imposed by people or conditions outside of you. Develop an awareness of the factors that may be interfering with your ability to complete your work.

Protecting Your Time

Your time is a valuable commodity. In order to protect the time your business requires, you may need to be more assertive by not allowing people to "steal" time away from you. List the people who "steal" time from you and the development of your business and how they do this:

People Who "Steal" Time	How They Do It
_____	_____
_____	_____
_____	_____
_____	_____
_____	_____
_____	_____

Protecting your time from unnecessary activities also is critical in being a good time manager and business owner. What can you do to protect your time? Complete your answers below:

Type of Time-Consuming Activitiy	How I Can Protect My Time
_____	_____
_____	_____

(continued)

Protecting Your Time (continued)

Type of Time-Consuming Activitiy (continued)

How I Can Protect My Time (continued)

_____   _____

_____   _____

_____   _____

_____   _____

_____   _____

_____   _____

Procrastination

Like many other prospective entrepreneurs, you probably have good intentions for starting your own business, but you can't seem to get around to just doing it. Rather than doing it, you spend a great deal of time and energy telling yourself all of the reasons why you cannot or should not begin your own business. If you are like many of the other would-be entrepreneurs who have great ideas that never get implemented, you probably listen to the endless tape that goes through your head with all of the negative reasons why you cannot succeed. When you do this, you get stuck focusing solely on how you will fail instead of moving yourself toward success.

Procrastination is a huge thief of time and one of the biggest blocks to entrepreneurial implementation and success. Procrastination occurs when you postpone unpleasant tasks or even things you want to do. You may have trouble getting started working on your goals, or you may have trouble finishing a goal because you get distracted or begin working on another goal. Although you might feel as though you need to rest before starting a task or that you work best when under pressure, pressure from undone tasks can cause stress in your life that is avoidable. You need to develop the habit of not procrastinating or else tasks will back up until you are unable to finish anything.

Answer the following questions to help you identify what you procrastinate about:

- What types of things do you put off doing?
- What keeps you from doing these things?
- What is the payoff for procrastinating?

If you still cannot identify why you procrastinate, you can use the following worksheet to identify other ways that you are procrastinating in reaching your goals.

Identifying Reasons for Procrastination

Putting off important tasks can be costly and can significantly hurt your chances of entrepreneurial success. You may procrastinate for a variety of reasons, such as fear of failure or concentration on day-to-day tasks such as responding to e-mail and telephone messages. Or, in your quest to accomplish the "big picture," you may put off frequent, important tasks such as networking for so long that it becomes nearly impossible to catch up. Use the following space to examine the reasons that cause your procrastination:

Reasons I Procrastinate	*What I Am Afraid Of*
Perfectionism	_____
	_____
	_____
Fear of making mistakes	_____
	_____
	_____
To avoid confrontation	_____
	_____
	_____
Feelings of being overwhelmed	_____
	_____
	_____
Other: _____	_____
	_____
	_____

Overcoming Procrastination

When you procrastinate, you are putting your life and career on hold because you are not ready to take positive action. Overcoming procrastination is about getting control of your time and accepting responsibility for taking action rather than blaming other people and situations for your lack of action. Try these steps for overcoming procrastination:

1. Write down a big task you need to complete to begin your business:

   _____

   _____

2. Break this task down into smaller tasks so that it does not seem overwhelming. List those here:

   _____

   _____

3. Ask your support system for help in overcoming your procrastination and completing your tasks. (Refer back to Chapter 2 for a list of these people.) List the people below who can help you and identify how they can help you.

   Person   *How He/She Can Help Me*

   _____   _____

                       _____

   _____   _____

                       _____

   _____   _____

                       _____

   _____   _____

                       _____

   _____   _____

4. Reward yourself. Provide yourself with small rewards as you reach your smaller goals. List ways you can reward yourself below:

_____

_____

_____

_____

Perfectionism

Perfectionism is the belief that you and everything in your environment must be perfect. It is a pervasive attitude that whatever you attempt in life must be done perfectly with no deviations, mistakes, or inconsistencies.

Examples of perfectionistic thoughts include the following:

"Everything must be done to my level of perfection."

"My level of competency is higher than most other people's level."

"I must always reach a level of perfection no matter what."

"I have no value unless I am perfect."

"The ideal is the only thing that matters, and if I do not reach the ideal, I am a failure."

"If I can't do it right, why even try?"

"I always need to be number one."

"What I achieve is more important than who I am."

If you scored low on the Perfectionism section of the Time Management Scale, perfectionist thinking may be a problem for you. You may tend to have inappropriate levels of expectations concerning yourself and others and develop intangible goals you can never achieve. You may feel unsatisfied regardless of your performance and achievements. You are likely to fear failing and making mistakes. This kind of attitude and belief can keep you from taking the risk to begin your business.

Overcoming Perfectionism

Follow these steps to overcome your perfectionism:

1. Become more aware of your perfectionistic thoughts.
2. Set realistic and flexible time frames for the achievement of your goals.
3. Forgive yourself for mistakes.

Think about some of the mistakes you have made so far in beginning your business. List them below and forgive yourself so that you can move on:

_____

_____

_____

_____

_____

From time to time, all entrepreneurs deal with time management problems. Successful entrepreneurs, however, have learned tools and techniques that allow them to either begin a business or continue to grow their business. A time management plan will help to ensure that your business tasks are being completed efficiently and effectively. The next chapter describes another important aspect in owning and operating your business: stress management.

CHAPTER 12

Manage Your Stress

Any entrepreneurial venture is fraught with personal and financial risk. Risk is part of the price that you pay as an entrepreneur to begin a business. Because of this risk, you will inevitably be forced to withstand long periods of uncertainty and stress. Starting and running a business is a constant battle between uncertainty and persistence, and living with the risk involved in starting and operating your business can affect your health. Your ability to be resilient through times of risk and manage the stress that comes with it is important to your personal wellness as well as that of your business. The better prepared you are to manage uncertainty and stress, the higher your odds become of being a successful entrepreneur.

Types of Stress

Entrepreneurs experience a variety of types of stress during the management of their business. Here are some of them:

- **Sensory deprivation:** The result of too little stimulation.

- **Stress overload:** The effect of too much to do in the time available.

- **Anticipatory stress:** Stress related to an upcoming change, challenge, or crisis.

(continued)

Types of Stress (continued)

- **Residual stress:** An aftereffect of a past event.

- **Build-up stress:** Stress that compounds over time.

- **Positive stress:** A motivator that helps in meeting deadlines, realizing full potential, and performing well under pressure.

- **Negative stress:** Stress related to an unanticipated event or crisis.

When you begin to experience stress related to your business, you will notice that you proceed through several phases before becoming able to cope with the stress:

1. **You encounter a stressor.** A stressor is a demand, circumstance, or situation that affects your equilibrium and evokes a stress response. Types of stressors include such things as anxiety, loss of a job, death of significant other, a lack of purpose, or noise.

2. **You perceive the stressor.** How important you perceive a stressor to be determines the effect it has on you. Each person evaluates stressors differently depending on their personal characteristics and past experience.

3. **You have a physiological response.** Based on your perception of the stressor, a variety of bodily responses occur that are external manifestations of the stressor.

4. **You manage the stress.** To do this, you can rely on a variety of different tools and techniques.

You need to build a stress management plan that is comparable to your business plan. This plan should include a variety of ways in which you will cope with the pressure associated with owning and operating your own business. To begin developing your stress management plan, it is critical that you explore your own wellness habits. Take the Stress Management Scale in this chapter to start and explore the techniques for effective stress management that are described in this chapter.

The Stress Management Scale

To be successful in handling the emotions associated with starting and growing a business, you need to be an effective manager of stress. The following assessment is designed to help you explore how effectively you are doing those things that naturally reduce the stress in life.

This assessment contains 30 statements related to your level of health and wellness. Read each of the statements and decide whether the statement describes you. If the statement does describe you, circle the number in the Yes column next to that item. If the statement does not describe you, circle the number in the No column next to that item.

This is not a test. Because there are no right or wrong answers, do not spend too much time thinking about your answers. Be sure to respond to every statement.

	Yes	No
1. I get enough sleep every night.	2	1
2. I am rarely irritable from a lack of sleep.	2	1
3. I have a regular sleep routine.	2	1
4. I do not keep myself fit.	1	2
5. I function well with less than eight hours of sleep per night.	2	1
6. I eat a lot of fast food.	1	2
7. I don't have time to exercise.	1	2
8. I maintain my appropriate weight.	2	1
9. I have difficulty falling asleep.	1	2
10. I consume way too many calories.	1	2
Section 1 Total: _____		
11. I get distracted easily.	1	2
12. I tend to be happy most of the time.	2	1
13. I adjust to change well.	2	1
14. I feel inner peace and contentment.	2	1
15. I express my emotions effectively.	2	1
16. I cope with stress in healthy ways.	2	1
17. I feel tired a lot of the time.	1	2
18. I take minor setbacks in stride.	2	1
19. I understand my own emotions.	2	1
20. I am optimistic about my life and my business.	2	1
Section 2 Total: _____		
21. I am open to new ideas.	2	1
22. I seek personal growth by learning new skills.	2	1
23. I am a negative person.	1	2
24. I use my business to seek mental stimulation and challenge.	2	1
25. I believe I can achieve my business goals.	2	1
26. I understand my strengths and weaknesses.	2	1
27. I let my negative thinking interfere with my business plans.	1	2
28. I look for ways to be creative.	2	1
29. I allow my thinking to make me sad.	1	2
30. I often think I am a victim of circumstances.	1	2
Section 3 Total: _____		

Scoring

This assessment is designed to help you identify your physical, emotional, and mental wellness as part of a stress management plan. For each section of the assessment, add the numbers that you circled in the Yes column to get a score for that section and write it in the Total line provided. You will get a total in the range from 10 to 20. Then transfer these totals to the spaces below:

Physical (Section 1) Total: _____

Emotional (Section 2) Total: _____

Mental (Section 3) Total: _____

Scores from 17 to 20 in any single section indicate that you have very effective wellness and stress management habits in this area. These habits will help you to deal well with the stress associated with owning and operating your own business.

Scores from 14 to 16 in any single area indicate that you have some of the wellness and stress management habits you need to deal well with the stress associated with owning and operating your own business. You need to continue to build these critical stress management skills.

Scores from 10 and 13 in any single area indicate that you do not currently have the wellness and stress management habits you need to deal well with the stress associated with owning and operating your own business. The good news is that you can develop these by completing the exercises in this chapter.

No matter how you scored, you will benefit from the information about stress management and the following activities.

Sleep Better

You can build your stress coping resources by getting enough sleep at night. Good sleeping patterns make a big difference in your health and how well you will deal with stress.

Exploring Bedtime Habits

Following are some bedtime habits you might explore to determine why you might not be sleeping well:

Bedtime Habit	What I Do	How I Could Do Better
Texting in bed	_____	_____
Reading in bed	_____	_____
Talking with friends	_____	_____

Bedtime Habit	What I Do	How I Could Do Better
Worrying about tomorrow	_____	_____
Watching television	_____	_____
Eating before bed	_____	_____
Working	_____	_____
Other: _____	_____	_____
_____	_____	_____
_____	_____	_____

Exercise Regularly

When you are in the midst of working in your own business, you will often find yourself filled with pent-up energy. It is important for you to learn ways to discharge your feelings physically (but in a healthy way) when you are feeling anxious and stressed. Regular exercise is one of the most effective ways to reduce the stress and anxiety associated with owning a business. Exercise also has been shown to reduce insomnia and depression and enhance feelings of well-being and self-esteem.

Aerobic exercise in particular helps the body by releasing chemicals, called endorphins, into your brain. When this occurs, your body is able to return quickly to normal, leaving you feeling refreshed and relaxed. Aerobic exercise uses sustained, rhythmic activity involving primarily the large muscles in your legs. Aerobic exercises include such activities as jogging, running, brisk walking, jumping rope, skiing, swimming, bicycling, kickboxing, any other active sport or high-intensity martial arts, and aerobic training. To maintain a minimum level of overall fitness, an average healthy person should participate in three 20-minute aerobic workouts a week, according to the President's Council on Physical Fitness and Sports (www.fitness.gov/fitness.htm).

In addition, your exercise program should include muscular strength and endurance activities, such as weight training and calisthenics, for about 20 minutes a day. Flexibility activities such as stretching (10 minutes daily) are an important component of overall fitness as well. As a general rule, space your workouts throughout the week and avoid consecutive days of hard exercise.

Remember that everyone should avoid inactivity, and entrepreneurs are no different. Some physical activity is better than none, and adults who participate in any amount of physical activity gain some health benefits.

Tracking Your Exercise

In the spaces that follow each of the physical activities listed, describe how often you participate in the activity each week. If you are new to exercising or to a specific activity, be sure to check with your medical doctor to make sure you are physically able.

Exercise or Activity	Weekly Minutes
Lifting weights	_____
Martial arts or yoga	_____
Hiking or walking	_____
Yard work or gardening	_____
Cycling or swimming	_____
Running or jogging	_____
Other: _____	_____

Eat Well

The relationship between nutrition and stress has been well documented. Certain foods and substances may create additional stress and anxiety:

Caffeine	Alcohol	Salt
Nicotine	Candy	Sugar
Red Meat	Soda	

Other foods tend to reduce the symptoms of anxiety and stress:

Fruits	Brown rice	Nuts
Vegetables	Fiber	Fish/Seafood
Water	Whole grain breads	Whole grain cereals

Improving Your Eating Habits

Answer the following questions:

What types of food do you want to eat more of?

_____

_____

What types of food do you want to eat less of?

_____

_____

What other changes do you want to make in your diet?

_____

_____

What positive changes can you make in how you eat (eat more regularly, eat more slowly, eat smaller portions, etc.)?

_____

_____

Relax

Although a little bit of stress can be helpful in building your business, stress can become overwhelming and throw your nervous system out of balance. When this happens, your nervous system is flooded with chemicals that prepare you for either "flight or fight." When this process happens too often, it wears your body and mind down.

For entrepreneurs who are experiencing stress, simple relaxation is often the best way to cope. For many people, relaxation means sitting in front of the television to forget about the stress of the day. Unfortunately, this type of relaxation has been shown to do very little in helping to reduce the negative effects of stress on the body, mind, and spirit. To effectively combat stress and the negative effects of stress, you need to find ways to activate the body's natural relaxation response. This relaxation response helps to bring your mind and body back to a state of equilibrium. You can activate your relaxation response by engaging in the following relaxation techniques.

Listen to Music

Listening to music can calm the most stressed-out entrepreneur. Because I find it soothing, I listen to music even when I am working on projects. If you think that listening to music can help reduce your stress, take a few minutes out of your day and try the following:

1. Put on the music you find relaxing and want to listen to.

2. Find and settle into a comfortable position and close your eyes. Allow your entire body to begin to relax.

3. Focus your attention on the music being played. If unrelated thoughts enter into your head, make a note of it and discard the thoughts. Allow all thoughts to disappear from your mind. You can use an affirmation such as "music relaxes me" to enhance your relaxation.

Do Progressive Relaxation

All entrepreneurs should take time to relax their bodies. Basic progressive muscle relaxation is easy to learn and it helps you to bring relaxation to all parts of your body through concentrated awareness. This relaxation helps to reduce anger and provides you with a system for stopping the escalation of anger in your daily life. Progressive relaxation allows you to produce relaxation by focusing self-suggestions of warmth and relaxation in specific muscle groups throughout the body.

Begin by sitting in a comfortable position. Close your eyes and start to feel your body relaxing. Think of yourself as a rag doll. Let the relaxation pass through each organ and body part. Start with your feet and progressively relax each part of your body. This will help you to manage your stress effectively.

Begin by having your body progressively relax with such statements as the following:

"I am relaxing my feet…My feet are warm…My feet are relaxed."

"I am relaxing my ankles…My ankles are warm…My ankles are relaxed."

"I am relaxing my calves…My calves are warm…My calves are relaxed."

"I am relaxing my knees…My knees are warm…My knees are relaxed."

"I am relaxing my thighs…My thighs are warm…My thighs are relaxed."

Do this with the rest of your body until you are totally relaxed from your head to your feet. Block any distractions out of your mind as you concentrate on relaxing your entire body.

Breathe Properly

You've probably heard someone tell another person who seems anxious or extremely stressed to "just keep breathing." This advice may sound crazy, but when you are experiencing high levels of stress, you breathe differently than you normally do. Your breathing generally illustrates the level of tension you are experiencing in your body.

When you are relaxed, you breathe fully and deeply, from your abdomen. It is virtually impossible to be tense and breathe from your abdomen. Abdominal breathing triggers a relaxation response in you. When you are tense, your breathing usually becomes shallow and rapid, occurring high in your chest. With this type of breathing, you tend to overbreathe and hyperventilate. You can retrain yourself to breathe deeply from your abdomen.

Breathing Through Your Abdomen

Inhale slowly through your nose, down as deeply as possible into your lungs. You should see your abdomen rise. When you have taken a full breath, pause for a moment and then exhale slowly through your nose or mouth. Be sure to exhale thoroughly.

Take 10 of these full abdominal breaths. Keep your breaths as smooth and regular as possible. As you continue this process, you can try slowing down the rate at which you take breaths. Pause for a second after each breath you take.

Tune In to Your Body

Sit back for a few minutes and tune in to the sensations present in your body. Don't attempt to change any of these sensations, just become aware of them. Pay particular attention to the parts of your body that feel tense. Now notice the parts of your body that feel relaxed. Remain focused on your physical sensations for a few minutes and make note of things that come into your awareness that have not been present before.

To effectively access your feelings, you need to shift the focus from your head to your body. To do so, try the following exercise:

1. Physically relax using mindfulness or meditation.
2. Ask "What am I feeling right now?"
3. Identify where in your body you are feeling the feeling.
4. Tune into the feeling to learn all you can about it.
5. Ask yourself "What is my main concern or problem?"

Think Positively

Entrepreneurs who are positive thinkers tend to see the glass as half full rather than half empty. They believe that the best is going to happen, not the worst. Positive thinkers have a mindset and an attitude in which they think that things are going to work out positively. Entrepreneurs who are positive thinkers naturally anticipate and always tend to foresee success, wealth, joy, and happiness as an outcome of every situation and action they take. It is critical for your entrepreneurial success that you understand and use the power of positive thinking. The following sections will help you to develop a positive thinking mindset.

Practice Mindfulness

Entrepreneurs tend to be effective at multitasking. This skill allows them to get a lot done, but it also increases the stress in their lives. Mindfulness can help entrepreneurs to be more attentive to the tasks at hand.

Mindfulness is that state of mind in which you are fully present with the person or the activity in which you are engaged. It is being in touch with the moment you are in so that you can see its fullness, hold it in your awareness, and come to know and understand it fully. It is being present in what you are doing at the time you are doing it. The type of attention associated with mindfulness increases your awareness and clarity and allows you to accept the reality of the present moment in a nonjudgmental way. When you lose awareness of the present moment, you create problems for yourself because you are forced to rely on unconscious and automatic thoughts and behaviors that have developed over the years.

Mindfulness is more difficult than it sounds. Many forces work against you being mindful during any activity. Some of these forces are the creation of your own mind and include attaching labels to your performance, rehearsing what you might say next rather than listening, thinking about other issues in your life, and judging yourself. When asked "Are you aware?" or "Where is your mind right now?" you will observe that your mind has a habit of trying to escape from the present moment. Remind yourself that this present moment is all there is.

Being Mindful

Stop for a moment. Sit down and become aware of your breathing. It doesn't matter for how long. Let go and fully accept the present moment. For several minutes, don't try to change anything, just let go and breathe. Breathe and be still. Give yourself permission to allow these moments to be as they are. Just let go and fully accept the present moment. If that does not work, focus your attention on any object for several minutes. Pick out an object and stare at it for several minutes.

One of the reasons your mind attempts to escape the present moment is the fear of being mindful. Your mind would prefer you to be thinking about the past, which you cannot control, and the future, which has not yet, and may never, come. Don't get caught up at this point in having a special experience or in making some sort of progress. You will slowly notice differences in your awareness over time.

Control Your Irrational Thinking

Entrepreneurs tend to worry about everything when it comes to their business. They feel a sense of ownership that is not felt by employees working for someone else.

Whenever you start to feel anxious or stressed about something happening in your business, try to examine your thinking by first stopping what you are saying and doing. Do not push your thoughts away or ignore them, simply stop in your tracks. Then think about what you are saying to yourself. Remember, what you say to yourself can either calm you down or make you angrier.

Do not say powerless, victim-affirming statements like these:

"Who is he or she to treat me like this?"

"Life's not fair."

"Just my luck."

"This is not right."

"This should not be happening to me."

"I don't deserve this."

"I can't do this."

Say powerful, self-sufficient, self-empowerment statements like these:

"I don't have to take this personally."

"They are entitled to their opinion."

"I will react differently this time."

"This is a challenge, not a problem."

"Life isn't always fair."

"These types of things can happen to everyone, not just to me."

"I can be a successful entrepreneur."

Monitoring Your Self-Thoughts

In the midst of running your business, you will have a constant dialog going on in your head, especially in times of stress. When you are in the midst of stress, a stream of mostly negative thoughts may invade your thinking. These thoughts can then lead to negative emotions. Think about a change you experienced or are currently experiencing and complete the table below.

Thoughts in My Head	Resulting Emotions	Result of These Negative Emotions
_____	_____	_____
_____	_____	_____

(continued)

Monitoring Your Self-Thoughts (continued)

Thoughts in My Head	Resulting Emotions	Result of These Negative Emotions
_____	_____	_____
_____	_____	_____
_____	_____	_____
_____	_____	_____

Sometimes you may need to simply stop the free-flowing negative thoughts in your head. Whenever you notice an anxiety or stress-producing thought entering your stream-of-consciousness, internally shout the word "stop" to yourself.

Stopping Negative Thoughts

Close your eyes and imagine a situation in which a stressful thought often occurs, such as talking in front of a group of people you do not know, going on a date, or going to a meeting at work. About 30 seconds after you begin to think about the situation, shout "Stop!" as the thought begins to enter your consciousness. Eventually, with some practice, you will be able to imagine hearing the word "stop" shouted inside your head.

Use Affirmations

Probably the best tool for you to use in quieting your critical mind is the use of affirmations. Affirmations are phrases you can use to reprogram your mind. These brief statements put you in the proper frame of mind to accept intuitive inputs. They are a way of sending your brain a message that the desired result has already been achieved. What you state, in the present tense, can easily be achieved. For example, you might want to use the following affirmations:

"I am handling the stress of starting my own business."

"My business is growing as I planned."

"I am managing stress well."

"Entrepreneurship is exciting, not stressful."

Reflecting on Affirmations

To strengthen your coping skills in stressful situations, you need to practice your affirmations on a daily basis. Select one of the previous affirmations that you feel comfortable with or create one of your own and repeat the affirmation for about five minutes each day for one week. An example might be "I have control over the stress in my life."

Write your affirmation here:

_____

_____

What observations did you make after doing this for one week?

_____

_____

_____

Balance Work and Leisure

As an entrepreneur, you may believe that you must abandon your leisure activities and spend all your free time working in order to make your business successful. However, it is important for you as a new entrepreneur to continue engaging in nonbusiness-related activities that you enjoy. By engaging in these activities you will find yourself experiencing less stress.

Ask yourself these questions:

- What types of recreational activities do I presently enjoy?
- What other types of recreational activities might help me reduce feelings of stress?

Finding more time for fun and relaxation can play a huge part in how you manage anxiety and stress. To assist you in being certain that you are doing enough to maintain a healthy and relaxed lifestyle, here are some suggestions.

At home:

- Give yourself time each day to rejuvenate and replenish your energy.
- Take a daytime nap if possible.
- Get enough sleep each night.
- Take time each day to stop doing things and simply rest.

- Devote time each day to your relationships.
- Be sure to take time each day to "be" each day, rather than "do." We are human "beings," not human "doings"!
- Take time to think.
- Don't feel like you must be productive each minute of the day.
- Spend time recreating.
- Spend time alone each day to reflect, read, and meditate.
- If you are a workaholic, learn to enjoy nonwork aspects of your life.

In your business:

- Prioritize work and differentiate between essential and nonessential tasks.
- Delegate work to others when appropriate.
- Allow extra time to complete tasks if possible.
- Set specific goals for completing projects and tasks.
- Know that it's acceptable if your work is not perfect at times.
- Do not leave tasks till the deadline.
- Be assertive and say "no" if you think it's the right thing to do.
- Manage your time as well as possible during the work day so that you have time left over for family and recreational activities.
- Remember that balance is critical for entrepreneurs.

When tasks that are related to time become stressful, it is usually because you are experiencing an imbalance among the various roles in your life. Think about the amount of time you spend on your personal self, your family self, your career self, and your relationships. It is important for you to develop an awareness of what is most important in your life.

Finding Your Work/Life Balance

Identify below how much time you are spending on various life aspects. Choose from the activities listed or feel free to make up your own. In this chart, identify how you are spending your time on a daily basis. List the activities on the chart and the amount of time you spend on a typical day on that activity. (Examples include exercise, work, intimacy, play/leisure, friendship, hobbies, community activities, solitude and contemplation, simple pleasures, household chores, eating, caring for children, caring for elderly parents, commuting to work, playing sports, playing/caring for animals, educational activities, reading, sleeping, and family activities.)

24-Hour Time Frame	Activities
7:00 a.m.–8:00 a.m.	_____
8:00 a.m.– 9:00 a.m.	_____
9:00 a.m.–10:00 a.m.	_____
10:00 a.m.–11:00 a.m.	_____
11:00 a.m.–12 noon	_____
12 noon–1:00 p.m.	_____
1:00 p.m.–2:00 p.m.	_____
2:00 p.m.–3:00 p.m.	_____
3:00 p.m.–4:00 p.m.	_____
4:00 p.m.–5:00 p.m.	_____
5:00 p.m.–6:00 p.m.	_____
6:00 p.m.–7:00 p.m.	_____
7:00 p.m.–8:00 p.m.	_____
8:00 p.m.–9:00 p.m.	_____
9:00 p.m.–10:00 p.m.	_____
10:00 p.m.–11:00 p.m.	_____
11:00 p.m.–12:00 midnight	_____
12:00 midnight–1:00 a.m.	_____
1:00 a.m.–2:00 a.m.	_____
2:00 a.m.–3:00 a.m.	_____
3:00 a.m.–4:00 a.m.	_____
4:00 a.m.–5:00 a.m.	_____
5:00 a.m.–6:00 a.m.	_____
6:00 a.m.–7:00 a.m.	_____

You also can reduce anxiety through small acts of kindness toward yourself on a daily basis. Allow yourself to make time each day to nurture yourself, away from your duties at work and home. When you nurture yourself, you begin to develop a loving relationship with you!

Nurturing Yourself

Some of the nurturing activities you can do for yourself are listed below. Place a check mark in the box in front of those you already do or plan to do and then list others on the blank lines.

☐ Take a long bubble bath   ☐ Get a massage

☐ Read an inspirational book   ☐ Take a walk

☐ Go to a matinee movie   ☐ Meditate

☐ Work on a crossword puzzle   ☐ Write in a journal

☐ Watch a sunset   ☐ Go to a local park

☐ Watch children play   ☐ Visit friends

☐ Rent and watch videos   ☐ Plant a garden

☐ Listen to your favorite music   ☐ Play with a pet

☐ Browse in a bookstore   ☐ Ride a horse

☐ Do yoga   ☐ Visit a museum

☐ Learn a foreign language   ☐ Drink a cup of tea

☐ Read a mystery novel   ☐ Play computer games

☐ Take a class   ☐ Play chess

☐ _____   ☐ _____

☐ _____   ☐ _____

Your Stress Management Plan

Most entrepreneurs are comfortable with both uncertainty and risk, but when these two factors build up over time they can cause tremendous levels of stress. In response to this problem, many entrepreneurs have begun to develop stress management plans to accompany their traditional business plans. You should do the same. Use the techniques presented in this chapter and the following worksheet to come up with a plan of your own.

Creating a Stress Management Plan

Fill out the following information.

Stress management techniques I have utilized in the past:

_____

_____

New stress management techniques I would like to try:

_____

_____

Steps I will take to begin using the new stress management techniques:

_____

_____

When and how I will practice these new stress management techniques:

_____

_____

Results I hope to achieve:

_____

_____

How I will know when I am successful:

_____

_____

If you are planning to start—or have already started—your own business, you know how stressful it can be. It's important to be aware of the effect such stress can have on your health and wellness. Take several of the tools and techniques presented in this chapter and make them a part of your day as an entrepreneur. Your health and the health of your business will thrive.

Business Ideas and Resources for Entrepreneurs

To get your entrepreneurial ideas flowing, this appendix lists and describes some common small businesses in different areas of interest that you might not have considered. It also points you to websites and organizations that can provide more information. Once you have a business idea, consult the general resources listed at the end of this appendix for advice and information on how to implement your idea.

Business Ideas by Career Cluster

Following is a partial list of some of the potential business ideas categorized into the 16 career clusters used in Chapter 4 and Chapter 5. Use this list as a starting point for generating your own business ideas. Some of the clusters feature sample job descriptions that come from information gathered by the U.S. Department of Labor's Bureau of Labor Statistics. These job descriptions provide insight into the self-employment opportunities for a variety of occupations. More information on these and other occupations is available in the *Occupational Outlook Handbook*, available in book form from JIST Publishing or online at www.bls.gov/oco.

Agriculture and Natural Resources

If you enjoy working with plants or animals, one of these business ideas may work for you.

- **Landscape contractor:** People in this business create new functional outdoor areas and upgrade existing landscapes but also may help maintain landscapes. Their duties include planting bushes, trees, sod, and other forms of vegetation; edging; trimming; fertilizing; watering; and mulching lawns and grounds. They also grade property by creating or smoothing hills and inclines; install lighting or sprinkler systems; and build walkways, terraces, patios, decks, and fountains. They provide their services in a variety of residential and commercial settings, such as homes, apartment buildings, office buildings, shopping malls, and hotels and motels. For more information, contact the Professional Landcare Network at www.landcarenetwork.org.

- **Pet sitter:** People in this type of business look after one or more animals when the owner is away. They do this by traveling to the pet owner's home to carry out the daily routine. Most pet sitters feed, walk, and play with the animals, but some more experienced sitters also may be required to bathe, train, or groom them. Most watch over dogs and a few take care of cats. Pet sitters are not required to have any specific training, but knowledge of and some form of previous experience with animals often are recommended. The National Association of Professional Pet Sitters (www.petsitters.org) offers a certification program that includes topics such as business management and animal health issues.

Other business ideas include animal show judge, animal trainer, aquaculturist, arborist, artificial animal inseminator, beekeeper, bonsai tree grower, butterfly breeder, Christmas tree grower, commercial fisherman, dog walker, environmental consultant, exotic animal breeder, farmer, fish farmer, fishing guide, fishing information broker, fruit tree grower, game bird breeder, garden designer, grass painter, green business owner, herb grower, horse breeder, horse exerciser, horse trainer, horseback riding instructor, horticulturist, hunting guide, landscaping service provider, lawn care service, livestock broker, llama breeder, lost pet locator, mobile pet groomer, nursery grower, orchid grower, pet groomer, pet ID service provider, pet supply retailer, pet taxi service, pet therapist, river rafting guide, sod service provider, taxidermist, tree planter, tree pruner, and tree remover.

Architecture and Construction

The following business ideas relate to the development and maintenance of buildings and other structures.

- **Home inspector:** People in this type of business conduct inspections of newly built or previously owned homes, condominiums, townhomes, manufactured homes, apartments, and commercial buildings. Home inspectors are most often hired by prospective home buyers to inspect and report on the condition of a home's systems, components, and structure. Although they look for and report violations of building codes, they do not have the power to enforce compliance with the codes. Typically, they are hired either immediately prior to a purchase offer on a home or as a contingency to a sales contract. Some home inspections are done for homeowners who want an evaluation of their home's condition, for example, prior to putting the home on the market or as a way to diagnose problems. For information about becoming a home inspector, contact either the American Society of Home Inspectors (www.ashi.org) or the National Association of Home Inspectors (www.nahi.org).

- **Interior designer:** Interior designers draw upon many disciplines to enhance the function, safety, and aesthetics of interior spaces. Their main concerns are with how different colors, textures, furniture, lighting, and space work together to meet the needs of a building's occupants. Some interior designers choose to specialize in one design element to create a niche for themselves in an increasingly competitive market. For example, the demand for kitchen and bath design, home theater design, conference facility design, outdoor living space design, ergonomic design, and green design are all expected to increase. For residential design projects, self-employed interior designers usually earn a per-hour consulting fee, plus a percentage of the total cost of furniture, lighting, artwork, and other design elements. For commercial projects, they might charge a per-hour consulting fee, charge by the square footage, or charge a flat fee for the whole project. Also, designers who use specialty contractors usually earn a percentage of the contractor's earnings on the project in return for hiring the contractor. For more information, contact the American Society of Interior Designers at www.asid.org.

Other business ideas include architect, architectural designer, architectural model maker, architectural salvager, asbestos remover, assayer birdhouse builder, cabinet maker, carpenter, construction site clean-up service provider, contractor, doghouse builder, electrician, floor installer, furniture maker, furniture restorer, hardware store owner, historic preservation specialist, home remodeler, home renovating service, home stager, house painter, interior decorator, landscape architect, mason, plasterer, plumber, restoration specialist, roofer, and stonemason.

Arts and Communication

Many professionals in the arts and communication career cluster are fully self-employed or take on occasional freelance work. Competition can be tough in these creative fields, but if you have the talent and the drive, you can create a successful business.

- **Photographer:** More than half of all photographers are self-employed, a much higher proportion than for most occupations. To create commercial-quality photographs, photographers need technical expertise, creativity, and the appropriate professional equipment. Self-employed, or freelance, photographers usually specialize in one field, such as portrait, commercial and industrial, scientific, news, or fine arts photography. Most photographers spend only a small portion of their work schedule actually taking photographs. Their most common activities are editing images on a computer and looking for new business. In addition to carrying out assignments under direct contract with clients, they may license the use of their photographs through stock-photo agencies or market their work directly to the public. Photographers who operate their own business, or freelance, must know how to prepare a business plan; submit bids; write contracts; keep financial records; market their work; hire models, if needed; get permission to shoot on locations that normally are not open to the public; obtain releases to use photographs of people; and license and price photographs. To protect their rights and their work, self-employed photographers require basic knowledge of licensing and copyright laws, as well as knowledge of contracts and negotiation procedures. For more information, contact Professional Photographers of America at www.ppa.com.

- **Writer:** About 70 percent of writers and authors are self-employed. They make their living by selling their written content to book and magazine publishers; news organizations; advertising agencies; or movie, theater, or television producers or by working under contract with an organization. The ability to send e-mail or text messages, transmit and download stories, perform research, or review materials using the Internet allows writers greater flexibility in where and how they complete assignments. Laptop computers and wireless communications technologies allow growing numbers of writers and authors to work from home and on the road. Still, some writers and authors work in offices and many travel to conduct on-site research on their topic. Many writers are paid per assignment; therefore, they work any number of hours necessary to meet a deadline. As a result, writers must be willing to work evenings, nights, or weekends to produce a piece acceptable to an editor or client by the deadline. For more information, contact the American Society of Journalists and Authors at www.asja.org.

Other business ideas include art consultant, art critic, art dealer, art gallery owner, art historian, art instructor, art repairer and restorer, art show promoter, art therapist, artist, blogger and affiliate marketer, bronze worker, calligrapher, candle maker, cartoonist, ceramic designer, choreographer, clothing designer, comedian, computer artist, creativity consultant, dance instructor, dance therapist, dancer, drama coach, event planner, florist, glassblower, graphic designer, home portrait artist, image consultant, jewelry designer, magician, mime, museum consultant, music teacher, musician, newsletter publisher, pianist, piano teacher, potter, proofreader, public relations specialist, puppeteer, scrapbooking service provider, silk screen printer, singer, and stained glass creator.

Business and Administration

There are many business opportunities in helping organizations to do their work more efficiently or complete specialized tasks, as in the following examples.

- **Management analyst/consultant:** People in this type of business analyze and propose ways to improve an organization's structure, efficiency, or profits. A high percentage (about 25 percent) of management consultants are self-employed, in part because business start-up and overhead costs are low. However, many small consulting firms fail each year because of a lack of managerial expertise and clients. Success in this field requires good organizational and marketing skills and several years of consulting experience. For more information, contact the Institute of Management Consultants USA at www.imcusa.org.

- **Meeting and convention planner:** People in this business coordinate every detail of meetings and conventions, from the speakers and meeting location to arranging for printed materials and audiovisual equipment. They travel regularly to attend meetings and to visit prospective meeting sites. They must be detail-oriented with excellent organizational skills, and they must be able to multitask, meet tight deadlines, and maintain composure under pressure in a fast-paced environment. Quantitative and analytic skills are needed to formulate and follow budgets and to understand and negotiate contracts. Planners also need computer skills, such as the ability to use financial and registration software and the Internet. About 6 percent of current meeting and convention planners are self-employed. For more information, contact Meeting Professionals International at www.mpiweb.org.

Other business ideas include abstracting service provider, book indexer, bookkeeper, business plan writer, carpet cleaner, cell phone accessory business, certified public accountant, collection agency, employee assistance program provider, employment agency, executive suite rental service, franchise consultant, grant writer, janitorial service provider, mailing list service provider, notary public, personal coach, private business consultant, professional organizer, property buyer, records processer, recruiter, relocation consultant, temporary staffing agency operator, trade show consultant, and training specialist.

Education and Training

If you have a passion for helping people learn, this business idea may work for you.

- **Child care worker:** People in this business nurture, teach, and care for children who have not yet entered kindergarten. They also supervise older children before and after school. In addition to attending to children's health, safety, and nutrition, child care workers organize activities and implement curricula that stimulate children's physical, emotional, intellectual, and social growth. About 33 percent of child care workers are self-employed, most of whom provide child care in their homes. Many states require child care centers, including those in private homes, to be licensed if they care for more than a few children. For more information, contact the National Child Care Association at www.nccanet.org.

Other business ideas include aerobics instructor, college applicant consultant, educational consultant, educational record-keeping system consultant, educational researcher, educational therapist, etiquette advisor, historical tour guide, homeschooling consultant, lifelong learning center administrator, preschool teacher or administrator, religious bookstore owner, sign language instructor, sign language interpreter, sports coach, teaching supply retailer, tutor, and vocational advisor.

Finance and Insurance

The following is a sample self-employment opportunity in this career cluster:

- **Insurance agent:** People in this business sell one or more types of insurance, such as property and casualty, life, health, disability, and long-term care. In addition to offering insurance policies, agents increasingly sell mutual funds, annuities, and securities and offer comprehensive financial planning services, including retirement and estate planning services, some designed specifically for the elderly. Agents must obtain a license in the states where they sell. Approximately 22 percent of insurance sales agents are self-employed. For more information, contact the National Association of Professional Insurance Agents at www.pianet.org.

Other business ideas include appraiser, bookkeeper, budget analyst, bulk food broker, certified public accountant, collection agent, debt counselor, estate planner, financial information service provider, financial planner, franchising consultant, fundraiser, income tax service provider, insurance broker, insurance consultant, insurance solicitor, investment counselor, investment manager, investment referral service, loan broker, mortgage broker, mortgage company owner, mortgage modification service provider, pawn broker, payroll processing service provider, retirement counselor, retirement planning consultant, SEC compliance advisor, tax preparer, and third-party insurance administrator.

Government and Public Administration

Business ideas include arbitrator, bartering business owner, campaign coordinator, collection agent, convention planner, curator, document shredding service provider, ethnographer, foreign correspondent, fundraiser, government surplus broker, lobbyist, mailing list service provider, mediator, museum exhibit designer, name creation consultant, notary public, office automation consultant, order fulfillment service provider, organizational historian, paging service provider, political campaign consultant, polling and surveying consultant, polygraph examiner, proofreader, public opinion pollster, reminder service provider, research analyst, survey developer, urban planner, and virtual assistant.

Health Science

The following is a sample self-employment opportunity in this career cluster:

- **Massage therapist:** Swedish massage, deep-tissue massage, reflexology, acupressure, sports massage, and neuromuscular massage are just a few of the many approaches to massage therapy. Because those who seek a therapist tend to make regular visits, developing a loyal clientele is an important part of becoming successful. Massage therapists must develop a rapport with their clients if repeat customers are to be secured. Because referrals are a very important source of work for massage therapists, networking will increase the number of job opportunities. Joining a professional association also can help build strong contacts and further increase the likelihood of steady work. Currently, about 57 percent of the people working as massage therapists are self-employed. For more information, contact the American Massage Therapy Association at www.amtamassage.org.

Other business ideas include acupuncturist, adult day care provider, aerobics instructor, aromatherapist, assisted living center owner, athletic trainer, diet counselor, dietician, funeral home owner, gym owner, health advisor, herb grower, home health care provider, hospice service provider, medical billing service provider, medical supplies retailer, nonemergency transportation provider, nutritionist, personal trainer, recreation therapist, specialty medical apparel salesperson, speech therapist, substance abuse counselor, technical writer, and yoga instructor.

Hospitality, Tourism, and Recreation

The following is a sample self-employment opportunity in this career cluster:

- **Hair stylist:** Hair stylists offer a wide range of beauty services, such as shampooing, cutting, coloring, and styling of hair. About 44 percent of workers in this field are self-employed. Many of these workers own their own salon, but a growing number of the self-employed lease booth space or a chair from the salon's owner. Hair stylists who operate their own salons have managerial duties that may include hiring, supervising, and firing workers, as well as keeping business and inventory records, ordering supplies, and arranging for advertising. Employment of hair stylists is projected to increase in the coming years by about 20 percent, much faster than average. This growth will primarily come from an increasing population, which will lead to greater demand for basic hair services. Additionally, the demand for hair coloring and other advanced hair treatments has increased in recent years, particularly among baby boomers and young people. The ability to attract and hold regular clients is a key factor in determining earnings. For more information, contact the Professional Beauty Association at www.probeauty.org.

Other business ideas include baker, bar owner, barber, bartender, bed-and-breakfast owner, brewer, cake maker, caterer, color consultant, closet organizer, clothing retailer, commercial kitchen supplier, cooking instructor, dating service operator, facialist, food safety consultant, food services provider, gift basket service provider, health food store owner, image consultant, lifestyle consultant, liquor store owner, make-up consultant, manicurist, organic farmer, party planner, pedicurist, personal chef, personal shopper, relocation consultant, restaurant owner, reunion organizer, specialty food manufacturer, sports bar owner, tattoo artist, tea/coffee shop owner, travel agent, wedding planner, weight loss counselor, and winemaker.

Human Service

The following is a sample self-employment opportunity in this career cluster:

- **Counselor:** People interested in counseling should have a strong desire to help others and should be able to inspire respect, trust, and confidence. Counselors frequently are challenged with children, adolescents, adults, or families that have multiple issues, such as mental health disorders and addiction, disability and employment needs, school problems or career counseling needs, and trauma. Education and training requirements are often very detailed and vary by state and specialty, but a master's degree usually is required to become a licensed counselor. A growing number of counselors are self-employed and work in group practices or private practice, due in part to laws allowing counselors to be paid for their services by insurance companies and to the growing recognition that counselors are well-trained, effective professionals. In fact, self-employed counselors who have well-established practices, as well as counselors employed in group practices, usually have the highest earnings for this occupation. For more information, contact the American Counseling Association at www.counseling.org.

Other business ideas include activity planner, camp consultant, career coach, career counselor, college admissions coach, companion service provider, e-coach, employment specialist, human relations counselor, interviewing coach, life skills instructor, marriage and family counselor, mediator, nonprofit ministry provider, nursery/day care operator, outplacement consultant, portfolio production service provider, psychosocial rehabilitation center operator, resume writer, safe home provider for domestic violence victims, and substance abuse counselor.

Information Technology

The following is a sample self-employment opportunity in this career cluster:

- **Computer software engineer:** People in this business analyze users' needs and then design, test, and develop software to meet those needs. The types of software include computer games, business applications, operating systems, network control systems, and middleware. Software engineers must be experts in the theory of computing systems, the structure of software, and the nature and limitations of hardware to ensure that the underlying systems will work properly. Software engineers with several years of experience or expertise can find lucrative opportunities working as systems designers or independent consultants, particularly in specialized fields such as business-to-business transactions or security and data assurance. These consulting opportunities should continue to grow as businesses seek help to manage, upgrade, and customize their increasingly complicated computer systems. Those with practical experience and at least a bachelor's degree in a computer-related field should have the best opportunities. For more information, contact IEEE Computer Society at www.computer.org.

Other business ideas include computer consultant, computer data recovery service provider, computer installer, computer repairer, computer security consultant, computer software consultant, computer software programmer, computer tutor, data processor, data storage facility owner, database maintainer, desktop publisher, digital imager, graphic artist, network installation and support technician, PowerPoint presentation designer, search engine optimizer, social media marketer, stock photography service provider, technical consultant, technical writer, trade show consultant, web author, web editor, web programmer, webmaster, website administrator, website designer, website host, and wireless phone service provider.

Law and Public Safety

The following is a sample self-employment opportunity in this career cluster:

- **Private detective:** People in this business assist individuals, businesses, and attorneys by finding and analyzing information. They connect clues to uncover facts about legal, financial, or personal matters. They offer many services, including executive, corporate, and celebrity protection; preemployment verification; and individual background profiles. Some investigate computer crimes, such as identity theft, harassing e-mails, and illegal downloading of copyrighted material. They also provide assistance in criminal and civil liability cases, insurance claims and fraud cases, child custody and protection cases, missing-persons cases, and premarital screening. About 21 percent of people working as private detectives are self-employed, including many for whom investigative work is a second job. Former law enforcement officers, military investigators, and government agents often become private detectives or investigators in a second career. Others enter from jobs in finance, accounting, commercial credit, investigative reporting, insurance, and law. These individuals often can apply their previous work experience in a related investigative specialty. In particular, opportunities for qualified computer forensic investigators are expected to be favorable. For more information, contact ASIS at www.asisonline.org.

Other business ideas include accident investigator, arbitrator, background checker, bail bondsperson, bodyguard, bounty hunter, collection agent, correctional consultant, credentials verifier, crime scene clean-up service provider, employment application checker, fire safety consultant, forensic reconstruction specialist, gun range owner, gunsmith, handwriting analyst, law office management consultant, legal transcriptionist, martial arts instructor, paralegal, polygraph examiner, private security operator, process server, safety equipment designer, safety trainer and consultant, security consultant, security dog trainer, security escort service provider, security specialist, and self-defense instructor.

Manufacturing

The following is a sample self-employment opportunity in this career cluster:

- **Home appliance repair technician:** People in this business install and repair home appliances such as refrigerators, dishwashers, washers and dryers, ranges, microwave ovens, and window air-conditioning units. In addition to making repairs, technicians keep records of parts used and hours worked, prepare bills, and collect payments. If an appliance is under warranty, a technician may need to confer with the manufacturer of the appliance to recoup monetary claims for work performed. Most home appliance repair technicians need to take periodic classes throughout their careers to keep their skills up to date and to be able to repair the latest home appliance models. Also, all repair technicians who buy or work with refrigerants must pass a written examination to become certified in proper refrigerant handling, as required by the U.S. Environmental Protection Agency (EPA). About 27 percent of technicians are self-employed. Those who are self-employed need good business and financial skills to maintain a business. Membership in a trade association can help business owners learn from others in the field. With sales of high-end appliances growing, demand for major appliance repair technicians should be strong into the future. For more information, contact the Professional Service Association at www.psaworld.com.

Other business ideas include air-conditioning mechanic, aircraft mechanic, audiovisual retailer, auto body repairer, auto glass installer, auto mechanic, avionics technician, car stereo installer, carpet salesperson and installer, CD manufacturing service provider, computer repairer, electronics installer and repairer, equipment broker, equipment sales representative, freight brokerage service provider, handyman, home appliance installer, home theatre installer, house painter, janitorial service provider, locksmith, piano tuner, refrigeration mechanic, toy designer, upholsterer, watch and clock repairer, and wireless phone sales and service provider.

Retail and Wholesale Sales and Service

The following is a sample self-employment opportunity in this career cluster:

- **Real estate broker:** About 59 percent of real estate brokers are self-employed. Unlike real estate sales agents, real estate brokers are licensed to manage their own real estate businesses. They often sell real estate owned by others; they also may rent or manage properties for a fee. Many real estate brokers work part-time, combining their real estate activities with other careers. Well-trained, ambitious people who enjoy selling—particularly those with extensive social and business connections in their communities—should have the best chance for success. However, beginning brokers often face competition from their well-established, more experienced counterparts in obtaining listings and in closing an adequate number of sales. Income usually increases as a broker gains experience, but individual motivation, economic conditions, and the type and location of the property also can affect income. Brokers who are active in community organizations and in local real estate associations can broaden their contacts and increase their income. A beginner's earnings often are irregular because a few weeks or even months may go by without a sale. The beginner, therefore, should have enough money to live for about six months or until commissions increase. For more information, contact the National Association of Realtors at www.realtor.org.

Other business ideas include advertising agency owner, advertising specialty sales provider, auction service provider, business broker, children's party planner, convention planner, copywriter, corporate speechwriter, dollar store owner, eBay reseller, estate sales manager, fundraiser, importer/exporter, insurance sales agent, jingle writer, mailing list service provider, manufacturer's representative, market researcher, marketing consultant, media and public relations business owner, promotional sales affiliate operator, real estate sales agent, sales product company owner, sales trainer, speaking coach, tourist services, used goods retailer, and used merchandise broker.

Scientific Research, Engineering, and Mathematics

Business ideas include archeologist, battery manufacturer, biodiesel research firm owner, computer technician, consulting engineer, economics researcher, educational game designer, energy consultant, engineer, environmental services consultant, equipment broker, freelance researcher, gemologist, geological consultant, invention consultant, patent consultant, product designer, recording engineer, recycler, renewable energy consultant, science recruiter, scientific consultant, scientific equipment repairer, speech pathologist, stress test engineer, technical writer, and veterinarian.

Transportation, Distribution, and Logistics

The following is a sample self-employment opportunity in this career cluster:

- **Taxi driver or chauffeur:** About 26 percent of taxi drivers and chauffeurs are self-employed. In many communities, drivers can purchase their own taxis or limousines and go into business for themselves. Independent owner-drivers need an additional permit allowing them to operate as a business. Individuals starting their own taxi companies face many obstacles because of the difficulty in running a small fleet. The lack of dispatch and maintenance facilities often is hard for an owner to overcome. Chauffeurs, however, often have a good deal of success as owner-drivers, and many companies begin as individually owned and operated businesses. For more information, contact the Taxicab, Limousine, and Paratransit Association at www.tlpa.org.

Other business ideas include accident clean-up service provider, airplane pilot, auto broker, auto customizer, auto detailer, auto repair/body shop owner, auto test driver, boat detailer, bus driver, car wash service provider, carriage driver, charter boat operator, charter bus business owner, children's taxi service provider, courier service provider, crop duster, driving instructor, flying instructor, handicapped transportation driver, limousine service provider, lunch truck operator, moving service company owner, muffler shop owner, small delivery business owner, tow-truck service provider, trash hauler, truck driver, valet service provider, window tinter, and windshield replacement service provider.

Resources for Entrepreneurs

The following are helpful resources for general information about entrepreneurship:

- **Count Me In** (www.countmein.org or www.makemineamillion.org): Count Me In is the leading not-for-profit provider of micro loans and business resources for women entrepreneurs. Apply to the Make Mine a Million $ Business Award program to get the assistance to grow your micro business to a million-dollar enterprise.

- **Entrepreneur** (www.entrepreneur.com): This magazine includes business ideas, the latest news, expert advice, and growth strategies for small business owners.

- **Entrepreneurship.org** (www.entrepreneurship.org): This free, international site from the Kauffman Foundation provides information of interest to individual business owners as well as those interested in policies and research related to entrepreneurship.

- **Enventys (www.enventys.com):** This company sells business services ranging from industrial design and prototyping to Internet marketing and public relations.

- **Everyday Edisons** (www.everydayedisons.com): *Everyday Edisons*, a PBS television show, introduces viewers to the process of invention and helps them understand how to take their own ideas to the next level.

- **FastTrac** (www.fasttrac.org): FastTrac is a practical, hands-on business development program from the Kauffman Foundation designed to help the entrepreneur hone the skills needed to create, manage, and grow a successful business. FastTrac participants don't just learn about business, they live it. They work on their own business ideas or ventures throughout the interactive program—moving their ventures to reality or new levels of growth.

- **Gaebler.com** (www.gaebler.com): This information website provides articles on topics of interest to entrepreneurs.

- **Inc.** (www.inc.com): This magazine specializes in small, high-growth companies. It includes sections on starting a business, writing a business plan, and buying a business.

- **Inventors Digest** (www.inventorsdigest.com): This magazine provides education and inspiration to independent and professional innovators.

- **IRS Small Business and Self-Employed Tax Center** (www.irs.gov/businesses/small): This site is where to go to apply for an Employer Identification Number. It also provides other small business tax resources.

- **Kauffman Foundation** (www.kauffman.org): The Ewing Marion Kauffman Foundation is the world's largest foundation devoted to entrepreneurship. It funds research to enhance the further understanding of the powerful economic impact of entrepreneurship and to develop programs that enhance entrepreneurial success.

- **Manufacturing Extension Partnership** (www.mep.nist.gov): MEP is a nationwide network of not-for-profit centers, in over 400 locations nationwide, whose sole purpose is to provide small- and medium-sized manufacturers with the services they need to succeed. Centers are funded by federal, state, local, and private resources to serve manufacturers. That makes it possible for even the smallest firms to tap into the expertise of knowledgeable manufacturing and business specialists all over the United States. These specialists are people who have had experience on manufacturing floors and in plant operations.

- **National Association for the Self-Employed** (www.nase.org): NASE is a resource for micro-businesses and the self-employed, providing a broad range of benefits and support to help the smallest businesses succeed.

- **National Venture Capital Association** (www.nvca.org): This website is designed to help entrepreneurs understand the importance of venture capital to the economy and support entrepreneurial activity and innovation.

- **SCORE** (www.score.org): The SCORE Association (Service Corps of Retired Executives) is a resource partner of the Small Business Administration (SBA) dedicated to entrepreneur education and the formation, growth, and success of small businesses nationwide. There are more than 10,500 SCORE volunteers in 389 chapter locations who assist small businesses with business counseling and training. SCORE also operates an active online counseling initiative.

- **Small Business Administration** (www.sba.gov): This website is the official U.S. government information resource for small businesses, small business owners, and prospective business owners. It offers information about such topics as loans and grants, taxes, regulations, international trade, government contracts, and disaster assistance. The SBA also provides small business counseling and training through a variety of programs and resource partners located strategically throughout the United States.

- **Small Business TV** (www.itsyourbiz.com): Small Business TV is a video news and information destination site for America's small business community. Its commitment is to provide small business owners with the resources and tools to manage, grow, and protect their ventures.

- **StartupNation** (www.startupnation.com): *StartupNation* is a website and nationally syndicated radio program focused on the nuts and bolts of entrepreneurship.

- **United Inventors Association** (www.uiausa.org): UIA is a resource for inventors/entrepreneurs seeking help in bringing inventions from garage to market. This educational nonprofit delivers expert advice, product evaluations, patent searches, news, and opportunities.

- **Women's Leadership Exchange** (www.womensleadershipexchange.com): The WLE mission is to provide the knowledge, the tools, and the connections women need to be successful in their own businesses, the corporate world, and the not-for-profit environment.

Index